P9-DWS-562

CALGARY PUBLIC LIBRARY

FEB   2018

ALL ABOUT DINOSAURS

ALL ABOUT DINOSAURS

ILLUSTRATIONS BY **ROMÁN GARCÍA MORA**

TEXT BY **GIUSEPPE BRILLANTE** AND **ANNA CESSA**

WSKids
WHITE STAR KIDS

CONTENTS

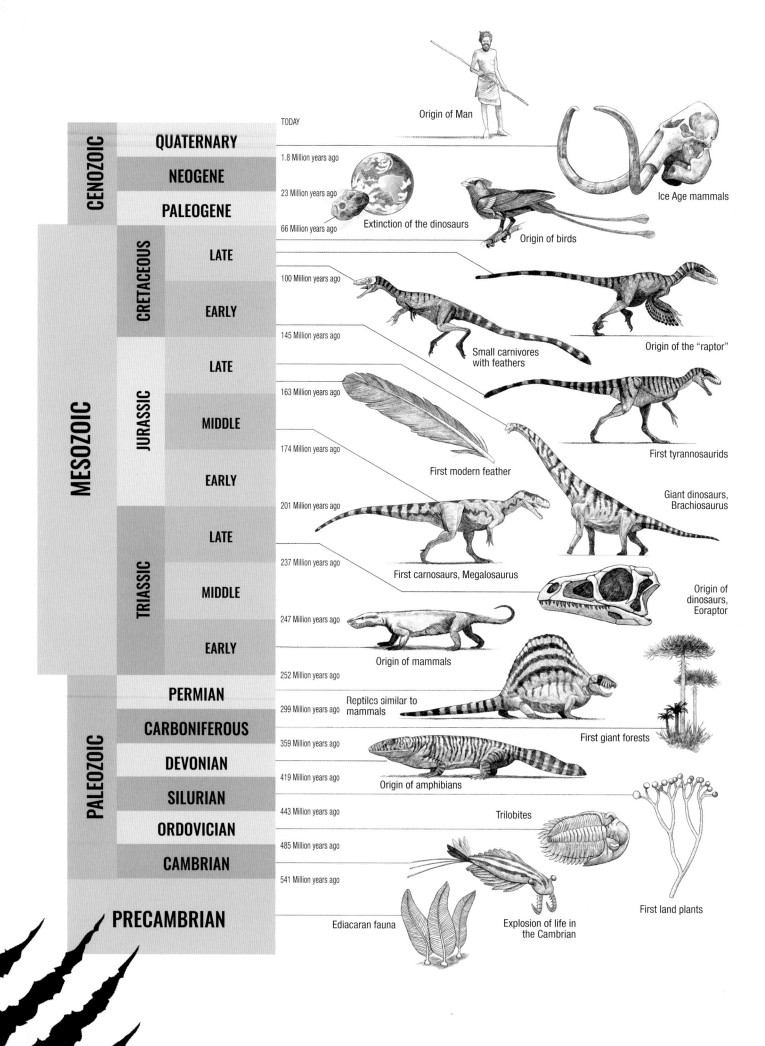

CENOZOIC

QUATERNARY

NEOGENE

PALEOGENE

MESOZOIC

CRETACEOUS
LATE
EARLY

JURASSIC
LATE
MIDDLE
EARLY

TRIASSIC
LATE
MIDDLE
EARLY

PALEOZOIC

PERMIAN

CARBONIFEROUS

DEVONIAN

SILURIAN

ORDOVICIAN

CAMBRIAN

PRECAMBRIAN

TODAY

1.8 Million years ago

23 Million years ago

66 Million years ago

100 Million years ago

145 Million years ago

163 Million years ago

174 Million years ago

201 Million years ago

237 Million years ago

247 Million years ago

252 Million years ago

299 Million years ago

359 Million years ago

419 Million years ago

443 Million years ago

485 Million years ago

541 Million years ago

Origin of Man

Ice Age mammals

Extinction of the dinosaurs

Origin of birds

Small carnivores
with feathers

Origin of the "raptor"

First modern feather

First tyrannosaurids

Giant dinosaurs,
Brachiosaurus

First carnosaurs, Megalosaurus

Origin of
dinosaurs,
Eoraptor

Origin of mammals

Reptiles similar to
mammals

First giant forests

Origin of amphibians

Trilobites

First land plants

Ediacaran fauna

Explosion of life in
the Cambrian

INTRODUCTION

DINOSAURS WERE THE UNDISPUTED RULERS OF THE PLANET FOR A LONG TIME. THEY BEGAN TO EVOLVE FROM PRIMITIVE REPTILES DURING THE TRIASSIC PERIOD, A GEOLOGIC TIME PERIOD THAT LASTED FROM 250 MILLION TO 210 MILLION YEARS AGO. THEY BECAME DOMINANT IN THE **JURASSIC PERIOD** AND CONTINUED TO BE SO UNTIL THE END OF **CRETACEOUS PERIOD**. DURING THE NEARLY HUNDRED AND FIFTY MILLION YEARS IN WHICH THEIR PRESENCE ON EARTH HAS BEEN VERIFIED, THEY ACHIEVED A PARABOLA OF SUCCESS. THEY GREW, THEY DIVERSIFIED AND THEY BECAME MORE AND MORE NUMEROUS. **THEN SUDDENLY, THEY ALL DISAPPEARED.**

SOME DRAMATIC EVENT THAT OCCURRED 65 MILLION YEARS AGO PUT THE WORD "END" TO THEIR HISTORY. **WHAT WAS THE CAUSE OF THEIR EXTINCTION?** *IT WAS PROBABLY A GIANT CELESTIAL BODY THAT STRUCK THE EARTH AT A SPEED OF 30 KILOMETERS PER SECOND.* THE HORRIBLE SHOCK WAVE AND THE DEADLY HAIL OF ROCKS RAISED BY THE IMPACT WOULD HAVE DEMOLISHED EVERYTHING WITHIN A RADIUS OF HUNDREDS OF KILOMETERS. THE REST OF THE DESTRUCTION WOULD HAVE BEEN CAUSED BY THE BLANKET OF DUST THAT FOLLOWED AND MADE THE PLANET DARK AND COLD. THE FIRST TO DIE WOULD HAVE BEEN THE LARGE HERBIVOROUS DINOSAURS, FOLLOWED BY THEIR PREDATORS, AND FINALLY WITH THE PASSAGE OF TIME, THERE WOULD NOT HAVE BEEN EVEN ONE DINOSAUR LEFT.

FOR HUMANS, THE DISCOVERY OF THE EXISTENCE OF DINOSAURS BEGAN WITH A FEW CLUES. A FEW FRAGMENTS OF BONE AND FOSSILS OF TEETH, FOUND BY CHANCE IN 1822 IN ENGLAND, SUDDENLY OPENED UP A PASSAGE TO THAT DISTANT PAST. SINCE THEN, **"DINOSAURMANIA"** HAS BEEN UNLEASHED.

FOR MOST PEOPLE, THESE HUGE BEASTS SEEMED TO COME FROM THE IMAGINATIVE MIND OF WRITERS. THE **"TERRIBLE LIZARDS"**, AS THEY WERE RENAMED IN 1841 BY BRITISH PALEONTOLOGIST RICHARD OWEN, WERE LIKE THE MONSTERS OF NIGHTMARES OR THE DRAGONS OF MEDIEVAL LEGENDS THAT HAD SUDDENLY BECOME REALITY. AND IT IS STILL THE SAME TODAY, AT LEAST IN PART.

HOW CAN YOU NOT FEEL A SHIVER RUN DOWN YOUR BACK WHEN YOU STAND IN FRONT OF THE SKELETON OF A **TYRANNOSAURUS REX** RECONSTRUCTED LIFE-SIZE IN A MUSEUM? IT IS IMPOSSIBLE NOT TO BE CAUGHT UP IN WONDER AND FEAR AT THE THOUGHT OF ITS FEARSOME CLAWS AND THE TERRIBLE BITE WITH WHICH THEY KILLED THEIR PREY. IT IS NO COINCIDENCE THAT HOLLYWOOD HAS TURNED THEM INTO THE LEADING STAR OF MANY MOVIES.

BUT HOW MANY **DINOSAURS** DO WE KNOW ABOUT? SO FAR, AROUND EIGHT HUNDRED SPECIES HAVE BEEN IDENTIFIED, **BUT IT IS ONLY THE BEGINNING**. NEWS OF DISCOVERIES OCCURS WITH A FREQUENCY THAT IS UNBELIEVABLE.

SOME **DINOSAURS** WERE THE SIZE OF A RABBIT; OTHERS WERE MORE THAN 45 METERS LONG.

THEY WERE LAND ANIMALS (PLESIOSAURS AND PTEROSAURS, WHICH LIVED IN THE SEAS AND SKIES, WERE NOT DINOSAURS) AND MANAGED TO COLONIZE EVERY PART OF THE PLANET. THANKS TO **ONGOING DISCOVERIES**, WE KNOW MORE AND MORE ABOUT THEM: HOW THEY MOVED AND HOW THEY HUNTED, HOW THEY TOOK CARE OF THEIR CHILDREN, AND WHO THEY SHARED THEIR HABITAT WITH. PIECE BY PIECE, PALEONTOLOGISTS ARE REBUILDING THE ENIGMATIC MOSAIC OF THEIR EXISTENCE.

THE CARNIVOROUS DINOSAURS

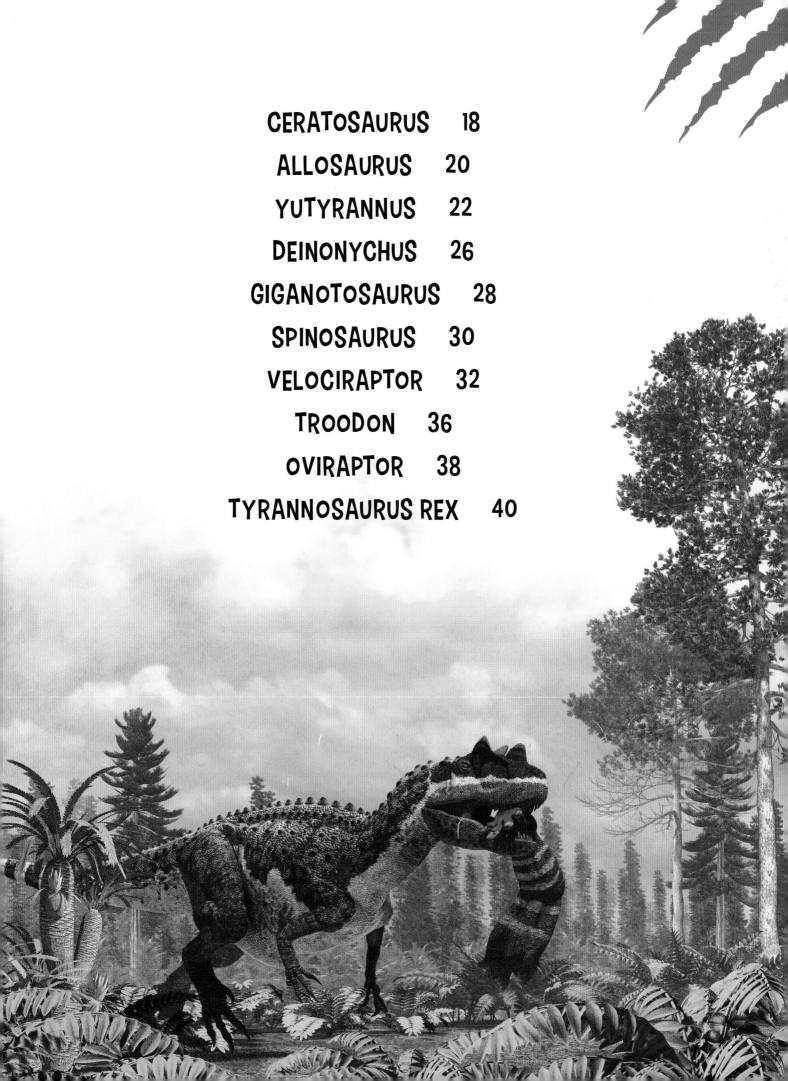

LETHAL PREDATORS

THE MOST WELL-KNOWN IS CERTAINLY **TYRANNOSAURUS REX**, A MONSTER AS LARGE AS A TRACTOR TRAILER WITH LONG DAGGER-LIKE TEETH. ITS ENORMOUS MOUTH, WHICH COULD OPEN UP AT AN ANGLE OF 80 DEGREES (THE ALLOSAURUS' MOUTH OPENED UP TO 92 DEGREES), ALLOWED IT TO SWALLOW PREY THE SIZE OF A HUMAN CHILD. **IT WAS THE EMBODIMENT OF TERROR**. BUT THOSE WHO THINK IT WAS THE LARGEST DINOSAUR PREDATOR THAT EVER EXISTED, ARE WRONG. **SPINOSAURUS**, REACHING UP TO 15 M IN LENGTH, SURPASSED IT. IT SCOURED SHALLOW WATERS IN SEARCH OF LARGE FISH WHICH IT CAUGHT WITH ITS CROCODILE-LIKE JAWS. ALTHOUGH THEY HAD SOME TRAITS IN COMMON (THEY WERE BIPEDS AND HAD COMMON ANCESTORS AS THEY ALL BELONGED TO THE **THEROPOD** GROUP), **CARNIVOROUS DINOSAURS WERE NOT**, HOWEVER, **ALL GIGANTIC**. ONE OF THE SMALLEST, **MICRORAPTOR**, ONLY GREW AS LARGE AS 80 CM AND WEIGHED JUST 1 KG.

IF WE ONCE THOUGHT OF THEM AS AWKWARD AND SOMEWHAT STUPID ANIMALS THAT HAD LARGE SCALES AND UNOBTRUSIVE COLORS, TODAY THE IDENTIKIT THAT PALEONTOLOGISTS MAKE OF DINOSAURS HAS COMPLETELY CHANGED. THE DISCOVERY OF CERTAIN FOSSILS SUGGESTED THAT SOME PARTS OF THE EARLIER DESCRIPTION DID NOT FIT. WHEN THE FIRST REMAINS OF A **DEINONYCHUS** WERE DISCOVERED, SCHOLARS BECAME AWARE OF THE **LARGE SHARP CLAW** ON ITS BACK WHICH IT USED TO WOUND AND KILL ITS PREY.

IN ORDER TO BE ABLE TO STRIKE WITH THIS DEADLY WEAPON, HOWEVER, IT WOULD HAVE HAD TO BE ABLE **TO MAKE GREAT LEAPS**, A BEHAVIOR THAT REQUIRED PHYSICAL CHARACTERISTICS THAT DID NOT SEEM TO FIT WITH THE IMAGE OF SLOW, COLD-BLOODED REPTILES THAT DINOSAURS HAD BEEN ASSOCIATED WITH THUS FAR. IT IS LIKELY THAT THE DEINONYCHUS **DID NOT NEED TO WARM ITSELF IN THE SUN** IN ORDER TO BECOME ACTIVE LIKE LIZARDS AND IGUANAS DO, BUT THAT INSTEAD, IT MAINTAINED A CONSTANT BODY TEMPERATURE, REGARDLESS OF THE CLIMATE WHERE IT LIVED, AND THIS MADE IT A RUTHLESS HUNTER.

BUT THIS WAS ONLY THE BEGINNING. THE MOST AMAZING DISCOVERY WAS THAT **MANY CARNIVOROUS DINOSAURS HAD FEATHERS**. ALMOST EVERY YEAR, NEW FEATHERED FOSSILS ARE FOUND ESPECIALLY IN CHINA. ONE OF THE LATEST WAS **YUTYRANNUS**, A DANGEROUS PREDATOR THAT WEIGHED OVER 1400 KG AND HAD AN INSATIABLE HUNGER.

BUT DID THEY KNOW HOW TO FLY? ALMOST CERTAINLY NOT. DINOSAURS USED FEATHERS TO LOOK MORE MENACING OR TO BE PLEASING TO THE EYES OF THE FEMALES THAT THEY HAD TO "CONQUER" DURING THE MATING PERIOD. THEY MAY EVEN HAVE USED LOVE DANCES TO ENTICE FEMALES, AS SEEMS TO BE INDICATED BY SOME ACROCANTHOSAURUS FOOTPRINTS IMPRINTED ON A ROCK IN COLORADO. AND EVEN **IF MOST DINOSAURS DISAPPEARED 65 MILLION YEARS AGO, SOME OF THEM**, BELONGING TO THE GROUP OF COELUROSAURIA THEROPODS, **EVOLVED INTO BIRDS** THAT POPULATE OUR FORESTS AND GARDENS. THINK ABOUT THIS THE NEXT TIME YOU BITE INTO A CHICKEN THIGH. ITS ANCESTOR WOULD HAVE TORN YOU APART!

CERATOSAURUS

WHERE IT LIVED:
North America, Europe, Africa

WHERE THE MOST IMPORTANT FOSSILS WERE FOUND:
Utah, Colorado (USA), Portugal, Tanzania

WHEN IT LIVED:
156 to 145 million years ago

SIZE:
up to 6 meters in length
and up to 2 meters tall

WEIGHT:
900 kilograms

With **its horns and its plates**, it looked just like a **DRAGON** from medieval legends. To date, no complete skeleton has been uncovered, but paleontologists are still able to give a "face" to Ceratosaurus, thanks to important discoveries made in the United States of America. It had **BIZARRE PROTRUSIONS** on its skull: a rather large nasal horn and two horns on its forehead. This is how it gets its name: "**horned lizard**."

Experts have long wondered about the function of these protrusions. According to some, they were **weapons used during the fighting** between members of the same species or against large predators. Others however, think that the horns were intended to **attract females** during the mating season.

or this reason, it is assumed that the **nasal horn could have had BRIGHT COLORS**.
Thanks to its long, flexible tail, Ceratosaurus must have been a **GOOD SWIMMER**, a bit like modern crocodiles, and probably hunted both in the water and on land. At its time, however, Ceratosaurus could have ended up as **prey for Allosaurus**, the large and fearsome carnivore that lived during the same period.

ANOTHER HYPOTHESIS ABOUT THE USE OF CERATOSAURUS' NASAL HORN IS THAT IT WAS USED BY THE SMALLER ONES TO BREAK THE SHELL OF THE EGG AT THE TIME OF HATCHING. THE NEWBORNS WERE PRECOCIOUS, LEARNED TO SWIM EARLY AND LEFT THE NEST A SHORT TIME AFTER THEIR BIRTH.

ALLOSAURUS

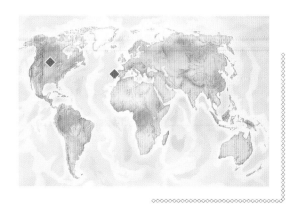

WHERE IT LIVED:
North America, Portugal

WHERE THE MOST IMPORTANT FOSSILS WERE FOUND:
Wyoming, Colorado (USA)

WHEN IT LIVED:
155 to 145 million years ago

SIZE:
up to 12 meters in length
and up to 4 meters tall

WEIGHT:
2 tons

Imagine the scene. An Apatosaurus flees while a fast **ALLOSAURUS** chases it. It is about to grab it and suddenly...the movie stops. Would it have caught and eaten it? We'll never know, because the evidence of that prehistoric drama is only found in a few **FOSSILIZED FOOTPRINTS** of the two animals impressed into the rocks in Texas.

Knowing Allosaurus' reputation as a **terrible hunter**, we can, however, assume that the Apatosaurus did not have a chance. Allosaurus was **the most common carnivore** in the Late Jurassic Period in North America. We have a pretty good idea of what it looked like thanks to **two almost entire skeletons** that have been preserved. One, known as **"BIG AL"**, belonged to a young dinosaur about 8 meters in length, now on display at the Geological Museum of the University of Wyoming. Its bones bear the **scars of at least 14 wounds**. One of these, on the right foot, had also caused an infection. The animal survived for a time, but then, probably unable to run and hunt like other Allosaurus, **IT DIED OF HUNGER AND EXHAUSTION**.

ALLOSAURUS OFTEN HUNTED LARGE HERBIVOROUS DINOSAURS. PALEONTOLOGISTS HAVE FOUND EVIDENCE OF THESE FIGHTS TO THE DEATH. FOR EXAMPLE, THEY HAVE FOUND THE VERTEBRA FROM AN ALLOSAURUS TAIL WITH A WOUND THAT CORRESPONDS TO THE SPIKED SHAPE OF THE TAIL OF A STEGOSAURUS, AND A BONE FROM THE NECK OF A STEGOSAURUS WITH SIGNS OF A BITE CORRESPONDING TO THE MOUTH OF AN ALLOSAURUS.

YUTYRANNUS

WHERE IT LIVED:
China

WHERE THE MOST IMPORTANT FOSSILS WERE FOUND:
Liaoning Province (Northeast China)

WHEN IT LIVED:
125 million years ago

SIZE:
9 meters in length
and up to 3 meters tall

WEIGHT:
1400 kilograms

Yutyrannus was only recently discovered and is the largest animal **WITH FEATHERS** that ever existed. It was a close relative of T-Rex. Though not as big as T-Rex, it was certainly nothing to fool with, as its 9 meters in length was **the size of a bus**. Do not be fooled by its good looks (its name, made up of Mandarin Chinese and Latin words, means "beautiful feathered tyrant") because it was a fast and fearsome **TWO-LEGGED PREDATOR**. Even though it had feathers, it could not fly. They were actually made up of simple fibers, more similar to the down of a chick than to the rigid feathers of an adult bird.

The feathers were most likely intended to **keep Yutyrannus warm**, given that at the time it wandered threateningly around the planet in the Early Cretaceous Period, the **CLIMATE** was relatively **COLD** (scientists have calculated an average temperature of around 10 degrees). It cannot be excluded that they also **helped it to blend** in with the environment so as not to be seen by its enemies or even the prey that it was hunting. They could also have been an ornament with which Yutyrannus **ATTRACTED THE ATTENTION OF THE FEMALES** during the mating season.

THE DISCOVERY OF A LARGE DINOSAUR WITH FEATHERS SUCH AS YUTYRANNUS PROMPTED SCIENTISTS TO ASK THEMSELVES ANOTHER QUESTION: IS IT POSSIBLE THAT EVEN T-REX HAD FEATHERS? SOME SCIENTISTS HAD ALREADY SUGGESTED THAT YOUNG T-REX DINOSAURS WERE ENDOWED WITH FEATHERS TO KEEP WARM, A PLUMAGE THAT DISAPPEARED IN ADULTHOOD. THE DISCOVERY OF YUTYRANNUS, A RELATIVE OF T-REX, BRINGS THE DISCUSSION BACK TO THE FOREFRONT. IT CANNOT, THEREFORE, BE EXCLUDED THAT ALSO THE LARGE AND FEARSOME T-REX HAD FEATHERS.

DEINONYCHUS

WHERE IT LIVED:
North America

WHERE THE MOST IMPORTANT FOSSILS WERE FOUND:
Montana, Wyoming, Oklahoma (USA)

WHEN IT LIVED:
118 to 110 million years ago

SIZE:
from 2 to 4 meters in length
and up to 1.5 meters tall

WEIGHT:
45-75 kilograms

The name **DEINONYCHUS** means **TERRIBLE CLAW**. It was named this by the two paleontologists who found its fossils during August of 1964. During an **excavation campaign in Montana** (USA), the two scholars saw a **GREAT CLAW STUCK IN THE ROCK**. They started to work on it and in a few days uncovered the remains of a dinosaur that had never been seen before. It was a small animal, certainly a carnivore, that walked on two legs using its long, robust tail to balance itself.

ts claw, located on the second toe of its hind legs, was a **deadly weapon**. It was thin and sharp and was used to inflict gashes and injuries to its prey after it jumped on them. Even its mouth was a strong weapon. With over **SEVENTY TEETH**, it was capable of a very powerful bite, almost **as strong as that of an alligator**. In conclusion, it was a fast, agile predator, that must have consumed a lot of energy, a factor that has sparked discussion among paleontologists: were dinosaurs cold-blooded or warm-blooded? If they were reptiles (the name **DINOSAUR MEANS "TERRIBLE LIZARD"**), they must have been cold-blooded (i.e. with a body temperature determined by their external environment).

Reptiles, however, are slow and clumsy, and must wait for the sun's rays to warm them up to take action. Deinonychus, however, was capable of rapid maneuvers during the hunt (it could reach up to **50 km in speed**) and had a behavior more similar to that of mammals and birds, which are warm-blooded. The debate has continued to this day and scientists are now convinced that **THE SMALLEST DINOSAURS WERE ALMOST CERTAINLY WARM-BLOODED**.

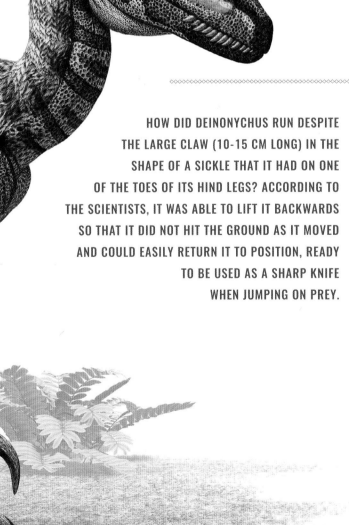

HOW DID DEINONYCHUS RUN DESPITE THE LARGE CLAW (10-15 CM LONG) IN THE SHAPE OF A SICKLE THAT IT HAD ON ONE OF THE TOES OF ITS HIND LEGS? ACCORDING TO THE SCIENTISTS, IT WAS ABLE TO LIFT IT BACKWARDS SO THAT IT DID NOT HIT THE GROUND AS IT MOVED AND COULD EASILY RETURN IT TO POSITION, READY TO BE USED AS A SHARP KNIFE WHEN JUMPING ON PREY.

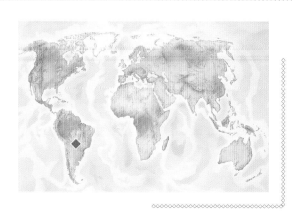

GIGANOTOSAURUS

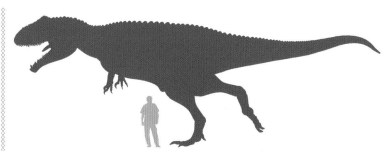

WHERE IT LIVED:
South America

WHERE THE MOST IMPORTANT FOSSILS WERE FOUND:
Patagonia (Argentina)

WHEN IT LIVED:
97 million years ago

SIZE:
up to 14 meters in length
and up to 7 meters tall

WEIGHT:
8 tons

It was a real prehistoric giant even bigger than **Tyrannosaurus Rex**.
It is not surprising that **GIGANOTOSAURUS** for a long time held the record
as the **LARGEST CARNIVORE** until it was moved to second place
by **Spinosaurus**. It moved on strong hind legs using its tail for balance
and searched for food in what is now South America. It is from this that
it gets its name which means **"GIANT SOUTHERN LIZARD."**

However, according to experts there is something that doesn't make sense. Although it was huge and had a head almost as long as a grown man is tall (even more than a meter and a half!), the power of its bite was much less than that of **T-Rex**.

It was certainly not able to kill prey rapidly; it is therefore possible that it was a **GIANT GARBAGE COLLECTOR** that fed on the carrion that it found, as hyenas do, and that it hunted like them in herds of more than one individual. There is even another problem: **IT WAS NOT PARTICULARLY INTELLIGENT**. Despite its very large head, its brain was small! It is estimated that it only grew to about the size of a **CUCUMBER**.

OUR KNOWLEDGE ABOUT THIS DINOSAUR IS THANKS TO THE PASSION FOR PALEONTOLOGY OF ARGENTINIAN **RUBEN CAROLINI**, AN UNEMPLOYED MECHANIC OF ITALIAN ORIGIN. ON JULY 25, 1993, WHILE HE WAS LOOKING FOR FOSSILS IN THE PROVINCE OF NEUQUÉN, NEAR THE VILLAGE OF EL CHOCÓN IN PATAGONIA, HE UNEARTHED AN ALMOST COMPLETE SKELETON OF THIS EXTRAORDINARY ANIMAL. WHEN SCHOLARS CHOSE THE SCIENTIFIC NAME OF THE SPECIES, THEY DID NOT FORGET HIM AND RENAMED IT "GIGANOTOSAURUS CAROLINII."

SPINOSAURUS

WHERE IT LIVED:
North Africa

WHERE THE MOST IMPORTANT FOSSILS WERE FOUND:
Egypt and Morocco

WHEN IT LIVED:
about 95 million years ago

SIZE:
15 meters in length
and up to 5 meters tall

WEIGHT:
7 tons

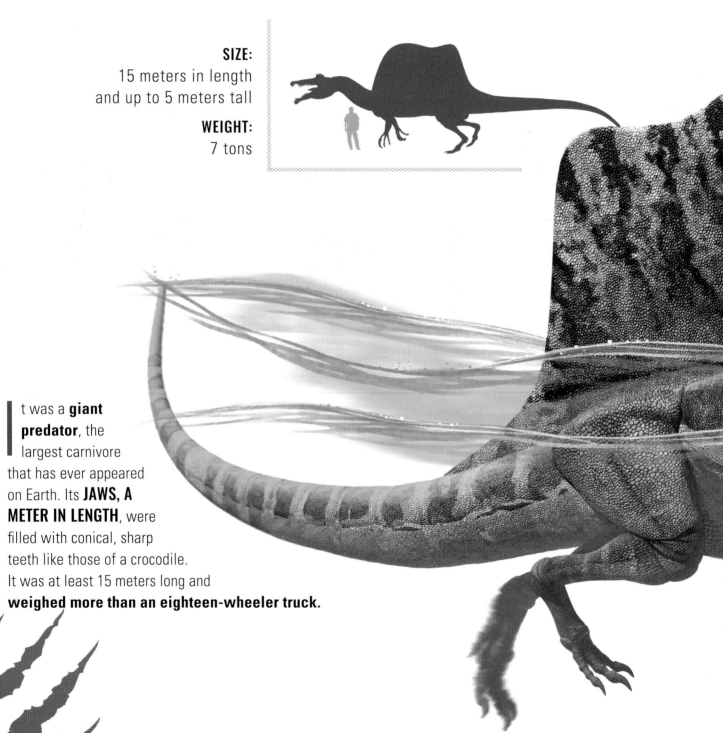

I t was a **giant predator**, the largest carnivore that has ever appeared on Earth. Its **JAWS, A METER IN LENGTH**, were filled with conical, sharp teeth like those of a crocodile. It was at least 15 meters long and **weighed more than an eighteen-wheeler truck.**

Along with the considerable dimensions, the lifestyle of Spinosaurus was also extraordinary: it is the only dinosaur that adapted to **aquatic life**. About 95 million years ago, it **SWAM IN THE RIVERS** of North Africa to hunt for giant fish that it caught with the **huge claws** of its front legs, moving using **hind legs that were probably webbed**. On its back was a **LARGE VEIL SUPPORTED BY THORNS**, which could reach up to 2 meters in height. The veil perhaps served to **attract females** during the mating season or to discourage other dinosaurs from invading its territory.

THE TWO MOST IMPORTANT INCOMPLETE SKELETONS OF THIS DINOSAUR WERE FOUND BETWEEN 1910 AND 1914 BY **ERNST FREIHERR STROMER** AND WERE PLACED ON DISPLAY IN THE MUSEUM OF MUNICH IN GERMANY. DURING THE SECOND WORLD WAR, AN AIR RAID DESTROYED BOTH THE MUSEUM AND THE TWO FOSSILS. FORTUNATELY, IN RECENT YEARS, OTHER EXAMPLES HAVE BEEN FOUND (THE MOST IMPORTANT FOSSIL IS PRESERVED AT THE MUSEUM OF NATURAL HISTORY IN MILAN) WHICH HAVE ALLOWED SCIENTISTS TO UNDERSTAND WHAT THIS PREHISTORIC GIANT LOOKED LIKE AND HOW IT LIVED.

VELOCIRAPTOR

WHERE IT LIVED:
Mongolia

WHERE THE MOST IMPORTANT FOSSILS WERE FOUND:
Gobi Desert (Mongolia)

WHEN IT LIVED:
85 to 71 million years ago

SIZE:
2 meters in length
and 50 centimeters tall

WEIGHT:
15 kilograms

When paleontologists saw the two fossils, they could not believe their eyes: they had unearthed a "snapshot" of a prehistoric drama. They discovered the **INTERLOCKED SKELETONS** of a Velociraptor and a Protoceratops: death had taken them at the moment they were fighting. Velociraptor had firmly seized the head of its prey and had wounded it with the **powerful claws** of its hind legs.

However, just when the fight seemed almost to have been decided, something unexpected happened. Initially, researchers speculated that the predator, after having thrust its claws so deep into its prey that it was unable to break free, was dragged by the bleeding Protoceratops into the water of a swamp, where they **BOTH DROWNED**.

Today, however, the dinosaurs are believed to have been covered by a sudden **LANDSLIDE OF SAND** as they struggled. In any case, they remained preserved like this, one on top of the other, for 80 million years, until they were unearthed in the Gobi Desert of Mongolia. It is therefore not difficult to understand why the "fighting dinosaurs" is one of the most famous fossils in the world.

VELOCIRAPTOR

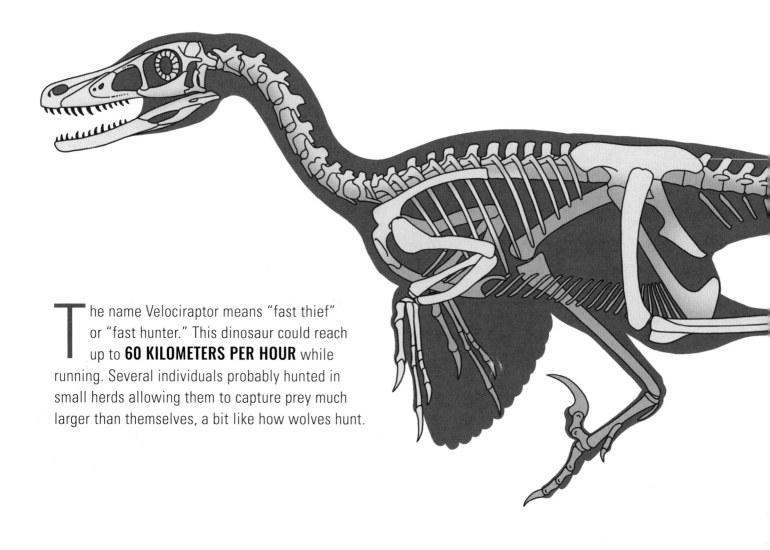

The name Velociraptor means "fast thief" or "fast hunter." This dinosaur could reach up to **60 KILOMETERS PER HOUR** while running. Several individuals probably hunted in small herds allowing them to capture prey much larger than themselves, a bit like how wolves hunt.

Although very often in movies and documentaries, the Velociraptor is **represented as "featherless"**, a specimen that showed the characteristic signs of feathers having been attached to the bones was discovered in 2007 in Mongolia. Researchers therefore concluded that Velociraptor was actually **ADORNED WITH FEATHERS ON ITS TAIL AND FORELEGS**. While not allowing it to fly, the feathers helped it while it was running and during mating rituals.

THANKS TO ITS CARPAL BONE (PART OF THE WRIST),
VELOCIRAPTOR WAS ABLE TO TURN ITS "HANDS" PREHENSILE,
MANAGING TO CAPTURE ITS PREY MORE EFFICIENTLY.
A FLEXIBLE WRIST IS ALSO AN ESSENTIAL FEATURE FOR FLIGHT
AND THE REASON THAT VELOCIRAPTOR
IS NOW CONSIDERED BY MANY SCHOLARS TO BE ONE
OF THE DINOSAURS WHICH DESCENDED FROM BIRDS.

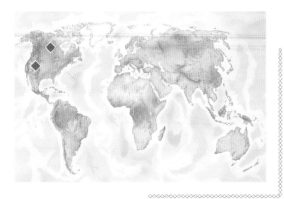

TROODON

WHERE IT LIVED:
North America

WHERE THE MOST IMPORTANT FOSSILS WERE FOUND:
Montana (USA), Alberta (Canada)

WHEN IT LIVED:
76 to 70 million years ago

SIZE:
2 meters in length
and up to 1.5 meters tall

WEIGHT:
between 40 and 50 kilograms

When it was found in 1985, paleontologists immediately realized that Troodon was a **special dinosaur**. It had a body almost two meters long, was equipped with legs that had an **OPPOSABLE FINGER ON THE FRONT LIMB** giving it a greater ability to catch its prey, and the **LARGE EYES OF A NIGHT HUNTER**. But its skull was the most impressive. This animal had a **brain three times larger** than that of other known dinosaurs at that time.

Therefore, if it had not disappeared as a result of the **mass extinction** that befell the dinosaurs, Troodon probably would have continued on an evolutionary path towards becoming an increasingly **refined life form.**

Paleontologist Dale Russell from the Canadian Museum of Nature in Ottawa, Canada, has tried to speculate what would have happened. According to him, Troodon dinosaurs could have developed into **INTELLIGENT BEINGS at almost the same level as man**. It would have had warm blood, an upright posture, a two-legged stride, and a **body covered with scales**. Over time, it would have **lost its reptilian tail**. It would have **cared for and fed its young** by regurgitating food. Finally, its big, round skull would even have allowed for **AN ADVANCED FORM OF LANGUAGE**. And there would have been no place for humans on the planet.

TROODON IS PROBABLY THE DINOSAUR WITH THE MOST WELL-KNOWN APPEARANCE, THANKS TO THE DISCOVERY OF MORE THAN TWENTY SPECIMENS. IN MONTANA (USA), EVEN ITS FOSSILIZED EGGS IN THE TYPICAL SHAPE OF AN ELONGATED DROP HAVE BEEN DISCOVERED. THE MOST SURPRISING PART IS THAT THERE WERE STILL EMBRYOS OF SMALL TROODON PERFECTLY PRESERVED WITHIN THEM.

OVIRAPTOR

WHERE IT LIVED:
Mongolia

WHERE THE MOST IMPORTANT FOSSILS WERE FOUND:
Gobi Desert (Mongolia)

WHEN IT LIVED:
75 million years ago

SIZE:
up to 2.5 meters in length
and up to 1 meter tall

WEIGHT:
25-30 kilograms

For a long time, this dinosaur was **considered a thief**. It was given this bad reputation by paleontologists when, about a century ago, they encountered its remains next to some eggs (**OVIRAPTOR** actually means **EGG THIEF**). However, this assumption did not correspond to the truth: in 1993, it was discovered that Oviraptor had been wrongly accused. Not only was it not a thief but it was actually a **LOVING MOTHER**. In the Gobi Desert of Mongolia, a specimen has been discovered from eighty million years ago which was perhaps **surprised by a sand storm** and died in an attempt to protect its nest and the eggs that it was sitting on.

The identikit of its appearance, taken from the bones that were found, shows us that it was an animal similar to a **LARGE OSTRICH**, almost as tall as a man, which ran fast on two legs. It had a **CREST** on its head, like that of cassowaries and **had a beak** instead of teeth, which functioned as a **SHARP CLAW**.

It probably used it to break the shells of shellfish, or to hunt small reptiles like lizards, which it captured with its **"hands" which had 3 fingers, equipped with curved claws** that were very sharp and eight centimeters long.

OVIRAPTOR IS CONSIDERED ONE OF THE DINOSAURS THAT WAS MOST SIMILAR TO BIRDS. ASIDE FROM BEING EQUIPPED WITH A SHARP BEAK AND NO TEETH, IT WAS ALMOST CERTAINLY COVERED WITH FEATHERS, LIKE MANY OTHER SMALL CARNIVOROUS DINOSAURS FROM THE LATE CRETACEOUS PERIOD. ITS PLUMAGE DID NOT ALLOW IT TO FLY, BUT WAS NEEDED TO KEEP ITS BODY WARM. THE TAIL FEATHERS WERE INTENDED TO ATTRACT FEMALES, LIKE THOSE OF PHEASANTS AND PEACOCKS.

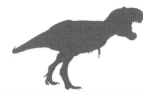

TYRANNOSAURUS REX

WHERE IT LIVED:
North America

WHERE THE MOST IMPORTANT FOSSILS WERE FOUND:
South Dakota (USA)

WHEN IT LIVED:
67 to 65 million years ago, at the end of the Cretaceous Period

SIZE:
up to 12 meters in length, and up to 5 meters tall

WEIGHT:
up to 7 tons

t is the most famous dinosaur. It even became a movie star. It is not surprising that it had a leading role in movies such as *Jurassic Park, Night at the Museum* and *Toy Story*, just to name a few. What made it into a celebrity? It was an extraordinary predator, one of the largest carnivores that has ever lived on our planet. Experts have long debated about the way that T-Rex (its name means **"TYRANNICAL LIZARD KING"**) procured its food.

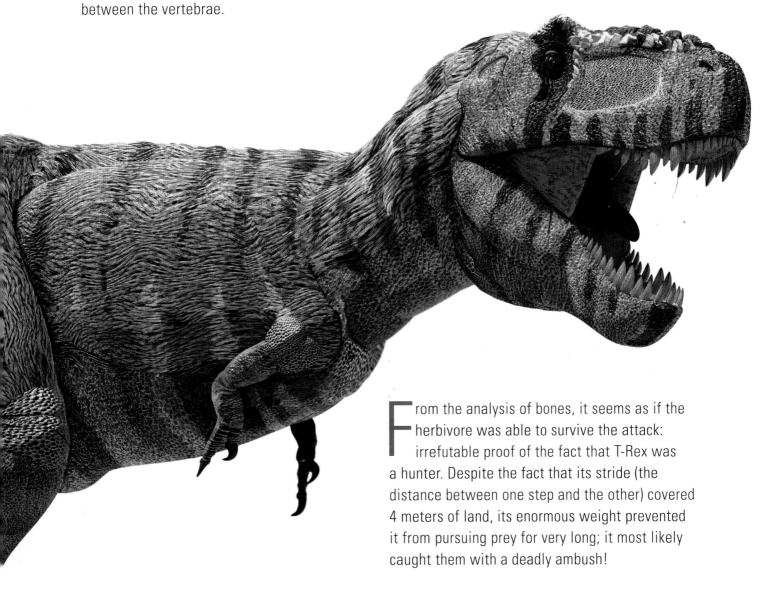

W as it a hunter who threw itself into the pursuit of prey or was it too slow to do so and therefore was a "garbage collector" who took advantage of the carcasses of the dead animals that it found? It certainly did not scorn at feeding on carrion, as many predators today also do, but in 2013, researchers at the University of Kansas in the United States discovered the fossilized tail of a Hadrosaur (a large herbivorous dinosaur with a beak like a duck) with a Tyrannosaurus Rex tooth wedged between the vertebrae.

F rom the analysis of bones, it seems as if the herbivore was able to survive the attack: irrefutable proof of the fact that T-Rex was a hunter. Despite the fact that its stride (the distance between one step and the other) covered 4 meters of land, its enormous weight prevented it from pursuing prey for very long; it most likely caught them with a deadly ambush!

TYRANNOSAURUS REX

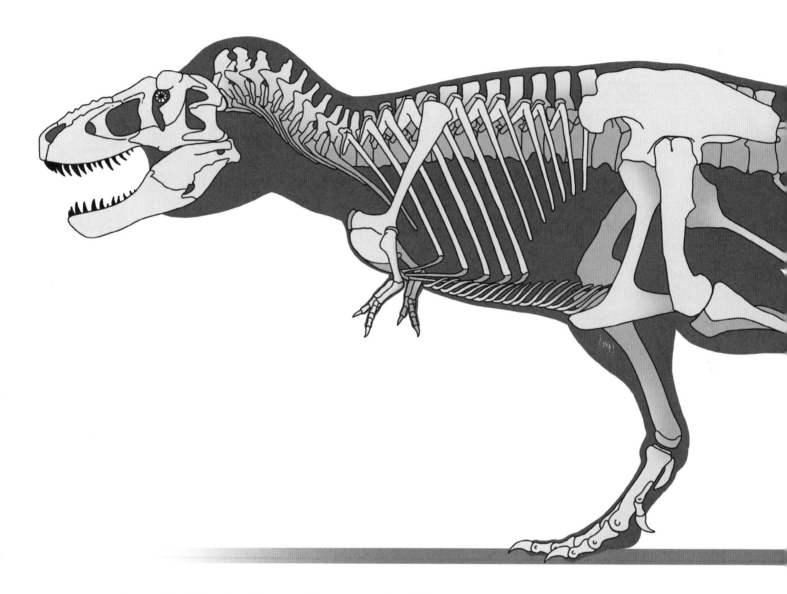

I t mainly fed on herbivorous dinosaurs and could swallow more than two hundred kilograms of meat in one bite. The power of its bite was so strong that the teeth penetrated the victim all the way to the bones, shattering them.

It had strong legs and a powerful tail that served to balance the enormous weight of its head (which was more than a meter and a half long). But above all, it was its mouth that caused people to shudder: it could open almost at a right angle and was "armed" with about fifty teeth that were 18 cm long, deadly weapons with which it seized, tore up and broke its prey into pieces.

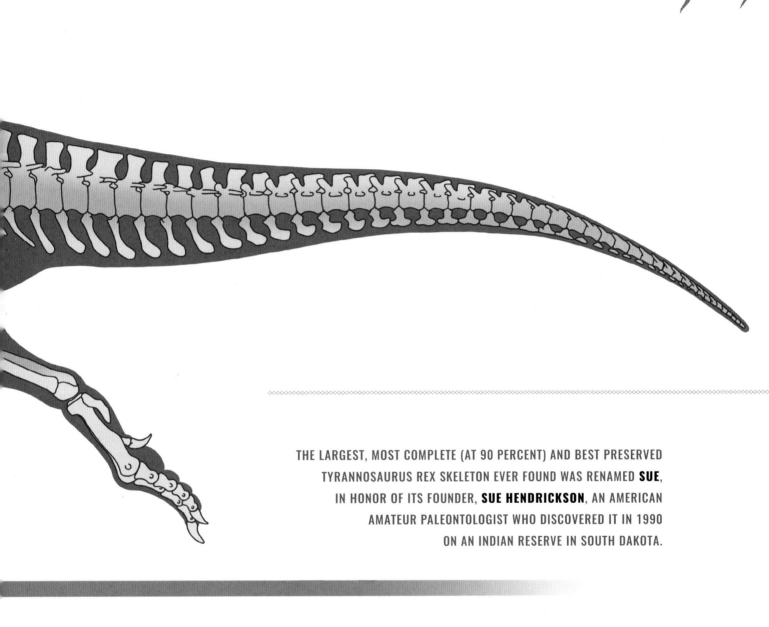

THE LARGEST, MOST COMPLETE (AT 90 PERCENT) AND BEST PRESERVED
TYRANNOSAURUS REX SKELETON EVER FOUND WAS RENAMED **SUE**,
IN HONOR OF ITS FOUNDER, **SUE HENDRICKSON**, AN AMERICAN
AMATEUR PALEONTOLOGIST WHO DISCOVERED IT IN 1990
ON AN INDIAN RESERVE IN SOUTH DAKOTA.

IT WAS OVER 12 METERS LONG AND MORE THAN 3 METERS TALL.
TO RECONSTRUCT AND ASSEMBLE THE OVER 250 BONES AND TEETH THAT
MAKE UP THE SKELETON TOOK MORE THAN 30,000 HOURS OF WORK.
ANALYSIS CARRIED OUT ON THE SKELETON DISCOVERED THAT IT DIED
AT ABOUT 28 YEARS OLD, A REMARKABLE AGE FOR A TYRANNOSAURUS
REX. TODAY IT IS ON DISPLAY AT THE FIELD MUSEUM OF CHICAGO, WHICH
PURCHASED 'SUE' FOR THE INCREDIBLE PRICE OF OVER 7 MILLION EUROS.

THE HERBIVOROUS DINOSAURS

"VEGETARIAN" DINOSAURS

EVEN THOUGH SOME OF THE MOST WELL-KNOWN DINOSAURS ARE CARNIVORES LIKE THE LARGE, FORMIDABLE T-REX, THERE ARE EVEN SOME **"CELEBRITIES"** AMONG THE **HERBIVOROUS DINOSAURS**.

STEGOSAURUS, WITH ITS LARGE PLATES AND TAIL OF ARMED SPIKES, WAS ABLE TO INFLICT FATAL INJURIES ON MORE AGGRESSIVE PREDATORS. **TRICERATOPS**, WITH ITS HORNS AND BONE COLLAR, LOOKED LIKE A REAL PREHISTORIC TANK. **MAIASAURA** INSTEAD WERE THOUGHTFUL MOTHERS, WHILE **OURANOSAURUS** WITH A LONG VEIL ON ITS BACK FRIGHTENED ITS ENEMIES AND WON OVER FEMALES DURING THE MATING SEASON.

FEW CAN COMPETE HOWEVER WITH THE WONDER BROUGHT ON BY THE MOST GIGANTIC OF THE **SAUROPODS**. **AS TALL AS FIVE-FLOOR BUILDINGS**, THEY WEIGHED ABOUT THE SAME AS TEN ELEPHANTS PUT TOGETHER. THEY WERE AMONG THE MOST IMPRESSIVE ANIMALS THAT OUR PLANET HAS EVER KNOWN. SOME OF THEM HAVE BECOME TRUE "STARS." THIS IS THE CASE OF **DIPLODOCUS**, THAT WITH ITS OVERLY LONG NECK, 6 METERS OF HEIGHT AND 16 TONS OF WEIGHT IS ONE OF THE MOST BELOVED AND ADMIRED DINOSAURS, ALONG WITH **BRONTOSAURUS** (OR APATOSAURUS, AS IT WOULD BE BETTER TO CALL IT).

THESE HUGE HERBIVORES (THIS DEFINITION IS NOT REALLY CORRECT, **IT WOULD BE BETTER TO DEFINE THEM AS "VEGETARIANS" BECAUSE GRASS DID NOT EXIST AT THE TIME OF THE DINOSAURS**, HAVING APPEARED ON THE PLANET ABOUT 40 MILLION YEARS AGO, WELL AFTER THEIR EXTINCTION) HAVE GIVEN SCHOLARS MORE THAN ONE PUZZLE TO SOLVE. **HOW**, FOR EXAMPLE, DID SUCH GIANTS **MOVE WITHOUT BEING CRUSHED BY THEIR OWN BODY?**

IT COULD NOT HAVE BEEN AN EASY OPERATION. THIS IS WHY IT WAS BELIEVED FOR A LONG TIME THAT ANIMALS OF THESE DIMENSIONS **MUST HAVE HAD AMPHIBIOUS PROPERTIES**: THE HYDRODYNAMIC PUSH GIVEN BY THE WATER WOULD HAVE BALANCED THEIR WEIGHT IN SOME WAY. TODAY WE KNOW THAT THIS WAS NOT THE CASE. THEY ALL LIVED ON LAND AND **THEY MOVED IN HERDS** (AS EVIDENCED BY FOSSIL FOOTPRINTS THAT HAVE BEEN FOUND) IN THE CONTINUOUS SEARCH FOR FOOD. THEY HAD **AN ALMOST INSATIABLE APPETITE**. IF AN ELEPHANT NEEDS 50 KG OF PLANT FOOD PER DAY TO FEED ITSELF, FOR THESE GIANT PREHISTORIC ANIMALS, ONE TON MIGHT NOT EVEN HAVE BEEN ENOUGH. BUT HAVING SUCH A CONSIDERABLE "SIZE" GAVE THEM SEVERAL BENEFITS. THE FIRST ADVANTAGE WAS TO HAVE PRACTICALLY NO NATURAL ENEMIES. EVEN **THE MOST AGGRESSIVE CARNIVORES**, AT THEIR HUNGRIEST, **RENOUCED AN ATTACK** ON THEM, DISCOURAGED BY THE IMPOSING MASS OF BONES AND MUSCLES OF AN ADULT HERBIVOROUS DINOSAUR. ONLY SMALL NEWBORNS, YOUNG OR SICK DINOSAURS SOMETIMES ENDED UP BETWEEN THE JAWS OF A PREDATOR.

SOME HERBIVOROUS DINOSAURS REPORT UNTHINKABLE RECORDS. **ARGENTINOSAURUS**, FOR EXAMPLE, WITH ITS 30 METERS IN LENGTH IS **PROBABLY THE LARGEST LIVING LAND BEING** THAT HAS EVER EXISTED AND THE SECOND LARGEST OVERALL (ONLY THE BLUE WHALE, WITH ITS 33 METRES IN LENGTH AND 180 TONS OF WEIGHT SURPASSES IT).

IN THE MILLIONS OF YEARS OF THEIR PRESENCE ON THE PLANET, DINOSAURS WERE ABLE TO FIND MANY SOLUTIONS TO HELP THEM SURVIVE. **HERBIVORES** WERE EXCELLENT AT THIS, BUT EVEN THEY COULD NOT ESCAPE THE CATACLYSM THAT BROUGHT ABOUT THEIR EXTINCTION.

PLATEOSAURUS

WHERE IT LIVED:
Europe

WHERE THE MOST IMPORTANT FOSSILS WERE FOUND:
Germany and Switzerland

WHEN IT LIVED:
214 to 200 million years ago

SIZE:
up to 9 meters in length
and 4 meters tall

WEIGHT:
up to 4 tons

Plateosaurus is a very old dinosaur and was one of the first to become specialized in **eating only plants** for food. We know a lot about its existence because more than **ONE HUNDRED FOSSILIZED SKELETONS** have been found, many of which are complete. We know, for example, that these dinosaurs moved around principally on their hind legs.

As a result of this and their **ELONGATED NECK**, this dinosaur could also reach the tallest branches of trees. We also know that it **lived on average between 12 and 20 years** because most of the specimens discovered were of this age (the oldest was 27). The strangest thing is that Plateosaurus came in **VERY DIFFERENT SIZES** and there were even some that could almost be defined as "dwarves": **some adults did not exceed 4 meters in length** while others reached up to 9. This was probably due to the **availability of food**. The smaller-sized animals were able to live in environments with limited resources.

MANY RECONSTRUCTIONS OF PLATEOSAURUS SHOW IT IN A FOUR-LEGGED POSITION, BUT A RECENT STUDY BY GERMAN PALEONTOLOGIST HEINRICH MALLISON HAS SHOWN THAT THIS IS AN ERROR. THIS DINOSAUR ACTUALLY HAD FRONT LEGS WITH THE PALMS LOCKED AND FACING INWARDS. IT COULD NOT THEREFORE HAVE ROTATED THEM TO LAY THEM ON THE GROUND AND WALK ON THEM. IT WAS THEREFORE CERTAINLY TWO-LEGGED.

STEGOSAURUS

WHERE IT LIVED:
North America, Europe, Africa, China

WHERE THE MOST IMPORTANT FOSSILS WERE FOUND:
United States of America, Portugal

WHEN IT LIVED:
156 to 150 million years ago

SIZE:
up to 9 meters in length
and over 2 meters tall

WEIGHT:
3 tons

Dinosaurs came in varied shapes and sizes, but Stegosaurus is one of the most extraordinary as a result of the **elaborate structure of its body**. What made is so uniquely identifiable were the **DOZENS OF PLATES**, some even one meter tall, **running in parallel lines on its body from its head to its tail**. What they were used for remains a mystery to paleontologists. There are many hypotheses: perhaps they served to **PROTECT IT AGAINST PREDATORS**, or served as signals during the mating season, when it was necessary for males to find strategies to show off for and attract females. But there are also those who argue that these plates were **FILLED WITH BLOOD VESSELS** and thus helped Stegosaurus **regulate its body temperature**.

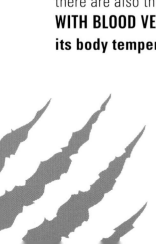

t had a very lethal tail, with **BONE SPINES** on the end that could be as large as one meter in length. Even though it was clumsy and slow, it probably more than compensated for its lack of agility with the **power of its blows**, as it was capable of inflicting mortal injuries on even the most aggressive carnivorous predators. **AS LARGE AS AN EIGHTEEN-WHEELER TRUCK**, Stegosaurus had to eat dozens of kilogram of vegetables each day to survive. Until recently, it was not entirely clear to scholars how these dinosaurs managed to procure such a large amount of food. **Grass had not yet appeared on the planet** and, different from other herbivores, Stegosaurus' narrow and elongated head that ended in a beak **DID NOT HAVE POWERFUL JAWS** or teeth adapted for grinding food. How did it then get enough food to survive considering all of these limitations? Recent research conducted by some British universities has shown that Stegosaurus had a **BITE** much more **POWERFUL** than imagined when considering the limited setup of its mouth.

STEGOSAURUS

According to researchers, its bite was **similar to that of sheep and cows today**: it was therefore able to also feed on leathery plants and not only on ferns and equisetum as was assumed up until a short time ago. Moreover, it is not entirely impossible that it had the ability to **rise up on its hind legs** using its **TAIL AS A SUPPORT** to reach higher vegetation, thus cutting out competition for food by other herbivorous animals that lived in its habitat.

THE MOST COMPLETE FOSSIL OF A STEGOSAURUS IN THE WORLD IS EXHIBITED AT THE
NATURAL HISTORY MUSEUM IN LONDON. IT IS 3 METERS HIGH AND 6 METERS LONG AND
WAS NICKNAMED 'SOPHIE' ALTHOUGH IT IS IMPOSSIBLE TO DETERMINE
IF IT WAS A MALE OR A FEMALE.

THE SKELETON, WHICH ACCORDING TO SCHOLARS IS 90 PERCENT COMPLETE, INCLUDES
MORE THAN 300 BONES AND 19 DORSAL PLATES AND WAS FOUND IN THE AMERICAN
STATE OF WYOMING IN 2003. WE KNOW THAT IT HAD TO HAVE BEEN A JUVENILE AND THAT
IT LIVED ABOUT 150 MILLION YEARS AGO, BUT THERE IS NO EVIDENCE PRESERVED THAT
HELPS UNDERSTAND THE CIRCUMSTANCES OF ITS DEATH.

BRONTOSAURUS

WHERE IT LIVED:
North America

WHERE THE MOST IMPORTANT FOSSILS WERE FOUND:
Como Bluff - Wyoming (USA)

WHEN IT LIVED:
155 to 145 million years ago

SIZE:
22 meters in length
and 8 meters tall

WEIGHT:
up to 20 tons

Brontosaurus is perhaps the best known dinosaur in the world, thanks to the animated film **"Fantasia" by Walt Disney**. It carries the reputation of being a slow beast, awkward and a bit stupid, with a gigantic body that could weigh up to 20 tons and housed a **BRAIN SMALLER THAN THAT OF A CAT**. Today paleontologists have changed this not-so-generous portrait, "painting" the picture of a successful animal (it was on our planet for a long period of time), **perfectly adapted to its habitat** and with **fairly developed social behavior** because it lived in herds. At the same time, they have also corrected another big misconception about this dinosaur. It was initially **ASSUMED THAT IT HAD AMPHIBIOUS HABITS** and passed much of its time with its body partially immersed in water in search of plants, a little bit like hippopotamuses do today.

All of these misconceptions were due to a simple but erroneous consideration. It was believed that the legs of this dinosaur were not able to withstand its enormous weight without the indispensable help of the buoyancy of water. Instead, we now know that its legs not only supported it perfectly, but allowed it to make **LONG JOURNEYS** in search of food and, when necessary, even to trot. It could **probably rise up on its hind legs** to reach the tops of the tallest trees. Brontosaurus was therefore an animal that moved on land, holding its **LONG NECK STRETCHED OUT PARALLEL TO THE GROUND**, a little above its shoulders, and balancing its weight with its **LONG WHIP TAIL**. The latter, if necessary, was an extraordinary **defense weapon**: one blow was capable of defeating even the largest carnivores such as Ceratosaurus and Allosaurus, which were its main predators.

THE MORE TECHNICALLY CORRECT NAME FOR THIS ANIMAL IS NOT BRONTOSAURUS BUT APATOSAURUS. THIS IS BECAUSE IT WAS INITIALLY THOUGHT THAT THERE WERE TWO SIMILAR SPECIES, BUT THAT THEY BELONGED TO TWO DIFFERENT GENRES. THEY WERE THEREFORE GIVEN DIFFERENT NAMES. THEN, AFTER A CLOSER STUDY OF THE FOSSIL BONES FOUND, IT WAS REALIZED THAT THEY BELONGED TO TWO VERSIONS OF THE SAME ANIMAL, AND THAT THE REMAINS OF THE APATOSAURUS WERE SIMPLY THOSE OF A YOUNG SPECIMEN OF BRONTOSAURUS. AS APATOSAURUS WAS FOUND FIRST, IT WOULD THEREFORE BE THE CORRECT NAME TO INDICATE THE SPECIES.

DIPLODOCUS

WHERE IT LIVED:
Western North America

WHERE THE MOST IMPORTANT FOSSILS WERE FOUND:
Colorado, Wyoming, Montana, Utah (USA)

WHEN IT LIVED:
145 million years ago

SIZE:
more than 30 meters in length
and 6 meters tall

WEIGHT:
up to 16 tons

It is one of the most gigantic dinosaurs that have ever lived on the planet. It almost certainly moved in **large herds that migrated seasonally** in search of food. **Fossilized** tracks of **footprints** have been found that seem to confirm this hypothesis and suggest also the dinosaurs' speed, or rather **THEIR SLOWNESS**: these mammoth animals went no more than 40 kilometers per day and only accelerated in case of need and for a very short period of time, reaching up to 20 km/h. On the other hand, one had to take into consideration their **CRAZY SIZE**, a feature that **was also an advantage** at a time when it was not difficult to become someone's prey. Due to their size, the adults of this type of dinosaur had virtually no natural enemies. Instead, it was the newborns and younger dinosaurs that ended up between the jaws of predators like Allosaurus.

With regards to defense strategies, it was long thought that Diplodocus used its **very long tail** (it was more than double the length of other sauropods) to deliver **DEADLY BLOWS TO THE ENEMY** when neccssary, but paleontologists recently became convinced that its tail was not suitable for hitting other dinosaurs because the impact of the hit would likely have fractured it. In 2004, a team of scholars from the American Geological Institute, making **RECONSTRUCTIONS** and carrying out computer **SIMULATIONS**, hypothesized that Diplodocus (as well as other large sauropods like Apatosaurus) was able to crack its tail as is done with a whip, producing a deafening noise like a cannon. Without having to make direct hits, it could **DISCOURAGE PREDATORS** keeping them away from the herd, as well as try to get noticed by females during the mating season. As for its appearance, scholars have recently revised their view of the appearance of Diplodocus, after the discovery of some traces of **fossilized skin** belonging to some of the specimens. They have added a **LONG RIDGE WITH SHARP SPINES** which ran along the whole body in the reconstructions, similar to that that is found on Iguanas today.

ACCORDING TO A STUDY DONE A FEW YEARS AGO, DIPLODOCUS SOMETIMES LOST A TOOTH WHICH WAS REPLACED QUICKLY BY A NEW ONE. IT HAPPENED ON AVERAGE EVERY 35 DAYS, WHILE FOR CAMARASAURUS, A GIGANTIC SAUROPOD WHICH RESEMBLED IT AND LIVED IN THE SAME HABITAT, THIS OCCURRED ONLY EVERY 62 DAYS. ACCORDING TO PALEONTOLOGISTS, THIS SUGGESTS THAT DIPLODOCUS FED ON VERY TOUGH ABRASIVE VEGETABLES AND THEREFORE USED UP ITS TEETH MORE QUICKLY THAN OTHER HERBIVOROUS DINOSAURS OF THE ERA.

AMARGASAURUS

WHERE IT LIVED:
South America

WHERE THE MOST IMPORTANT FOSSILS WERE FOUND:
Argentina

WHEN IT LIVED:
130 million years ago

SIZE:
9 meters in length
and up to 4 meters tall

WEIGHT:
up to 5 tons

It was one of the most bizarre-looking dinosaurs. **TWO ROWS OF BONE SPINES**, which were extensions of the dorsal vertebrae, ran in parallel along the top of its back, from its neck (where they were even more developed and could even reach up to half a meter in height) to its tail. One of the hypotheses about their function is that they were **COVERED WITH HORNS**. With these, the dinosaur would have had a weapon at its disposal against predators that attacked him. But not everyone agrees with this theory, as the position of the spines could only have offered a limited amount of defense. It would have been different if they had been distributed over the rest of its body. Given that **ONLY THE MALES POSSESSED THEM**, perhaps Amargasaurus used them to fight with rivals of its species during confrontations over females.

t is even possible that these spines supported **TWO SKIN "SAILS"**, useful for **regulating body heat** or intimidating enemies and attracting the opposite sex during mating season. They could also have been the support structure **OF LARGE KERATINOUS RIDGES**.

Although it was a sauropod like Apatosaurus and Brachiosaurus, it was a different size than they were. It had only **half the stature of its gigantic "cousins."** However, it did not pass unnoticed: it was almost as long as three cars placed one after the other.

DESPITE BEING A HERBIVORE, AMARGASAURUS DID NOT HAVE ANY TEETH THAT WERE SUITABLE FOR CHEWING FOOD. IT SWALLOWED THE PARTS OF PLANTS THAT IT ATE WHOLE, WHICH THEN ENDED UP IN ITS STOMACH WHERE THEY WERE GROUND UP WITH THE HELP OF STONES THAT THE ANIMAL INGESTED FOR THIS PURPOSE.

OURANOSAURUS

WHERE IT LIVED:
Africa

WHERE THE MOST IMPORTANT FOSSILS WERE FOUND:
Niger Desert

WHEN IT LIVED:
110 to 112 million years ago

SIZE:
up to 8 meters in length
and up to 3 meters tall

WEIGHT:
from 2 to 3 tons

Its appearance was truly unique as a result of the **LARGE "VEIL"** on its back that reached up to seventy centimeters. What it was used for is still a mystery. Maybe it had the function of **dispersing and accumulating body heat** or, more likely, it served the purposes of **DETERRING RIVALS** and getting noticed by the females that would only be courted by the specimens that exhibited the largest, strongest and most beautiful veils (they were **almost certainly also colored**). This is a strategy that some lizards and some birds use even today. These include the peacock that exhibits its enormous ornamental tail as a sexual call.

Some people, however, think that long dorsal spines, found fossilized along with the rest of the skeleton, **were not the framework for a veil**, but rather **A HUMP SIMILAR TO THAT OF CAMELS**, in which fat was accumulated that served as an energy store during times when it was more difficult to find food.

OURANOSAURUS HABITATS WERE THE DELTAS OF RIVERS. ITS MAIN PREDATORS WERE SUCHOMIMUS, A CARNIVOROUS DINOSAUR THAT WAS 10 METERS LONG, AND SARCOSUCHUS, A GIANT CROCODILE THAT REACHED UP TO 12 METERS LONG. THE FOSSIL REMAINS OF THESE ANIMALS WERE FOUND IN THE SAME AREA AS THOSE OF OURANOSAURUS.

EUROPELTA

WHERE IT LIVED:
Europe

WHERE THE MOST IMPORTANT FOSSILS WERE FOUND:
Spain

WHEN IT LIVED:
110 million years ago

SIZE:
5 meters in length
and up to 1 meter tall

WEIGHT:
up to 2 tons

Armored dinosaurs once **lived even in Europe**. In 2011, a specimen of **Europelta carbonensis** (the name refers to the **COAL MINE** where it was found) was discovered in Spain. Of it, however, not much is known, due to the fact that **no complete skeleton has been discovered**, but only the partial fossil remains of **two different individuals**. EUROPELTA, which was a medium-sized herbivore, belongs to a group of armored dinosaurs called **Struthiosaurinae** that were exclusively from Europe.

These dinosaurs, from the **NODOSAURIDAE** family, had a **rather narrow head** and a body that was not entirely covered with plates.
The **armor** of Europelta was actually not as thick and sturdy as that of other armored dinosaurs that came after it, but it was **still a good defense mechanism against predators**.
It lived in an area that was once **a coastal lagoon surrounded by forests and vegetation**.

THE NAME EUROPELTA COMES FROM THE JOINING OF THE WORD "EUROPE" (THE DISCOVERY PLACE OF THIS DINOSAUR, WHICH IS ALSO THE MOST COMPLETE ANKYLOSAURUS DISCOVERED THUS FAR ON THIS CONTINENT) WITH THE GREEK TERM "PELTA" WHICH MEANS "SHIELD" AND REFERS TO ITS ARMOR.

IGUANODON

WHERE IT LIVED:
Europe

WHERE THE MOST IMPORTANT FOSSILS WERE FOUND:
Bernissart (Belgium)

WHEN IT LIVED:
100 million years ago

SIZE:
10 meters in length
and 5 meters tall

WEIGHT:
up to 7 tons

In the late nineteenth century, some miners intent on digging a tunnel 300 meters underground in a coal mine in the village of Bernissart, Belgium, happened upon an **IGUANODON CEMETERY**. It contained at least thirty almost complete fossil skeletons. This discovery allowed scholars to obtain an accurate identikit of this herbivorous dinosaur. Iguanodon was mainly a quadruped, but in case of danger, could run on its hind legs, although it was **NOT PARTICULARLY FAST**, barely reaching 20 km/h.

This stance as a biped, which it also used to reach the highest branches of tree leaves and other plants that it fed on, was aided by a sort of **PREHENSILE LITTLE FINGER**.

In preliminary reconstructions, this dinosaur was portrayed with a **horn similar to that of a rhinoceros**. The discovery of the numerous fossil skeletons found in Belgium led to the realization that **THIS WAS AN ERROR**.

The bony tip was not a horn but rather the **claw of the first digit of the front legs** that Iguanodon used to defend themselves from predators, a sort of knife that it could use to inflict painful, deep wounds.

WHY WERE IGUANODON FOSSILS FOUND IN THE BERNISSART MINE ALL PILED TOGETHER? THE MOST LIKELY HYPOTHESIS IS THAT A SMALL HERD OF THESE ANIMALS, FRIGHTENED BY A PREDATOR, FLED INTO A DEEP GORGE WHICH THEN BECAME A DEADLY TRAP.

PROTOCERATOPS

WHERE IT LIVED:
Mongolia

WHERE THE MOST IMPORTANT FOSSILS WERE FOUND:
Gobi Desert (Mongolia)

WHEN IT LIVED:
110 to 70 million years ago

SIZE:
almost 2 meters in length
and 1 meter tall

WEIGHT:
180 kilograms

For the scientists who found them, it was like **looking at a photograph** that captures a moment of life on our planet from a distant era. Probably killed by a **POWERFUL SANDSTORM** that blew through the dunes of the Gobi Desert seventy-five million years ago, **fifteen young Protoceratopses** lay next to each other. The small dinosaurs, which were less than a year old, **were still in the nest.** Paleontologists have therefore inferred that **adults took care of the young**, fed them and protected them from predators for a **LONG TIME AFTER HATCHING**. This is clear evidence for **social behavior** by dinosaurs.

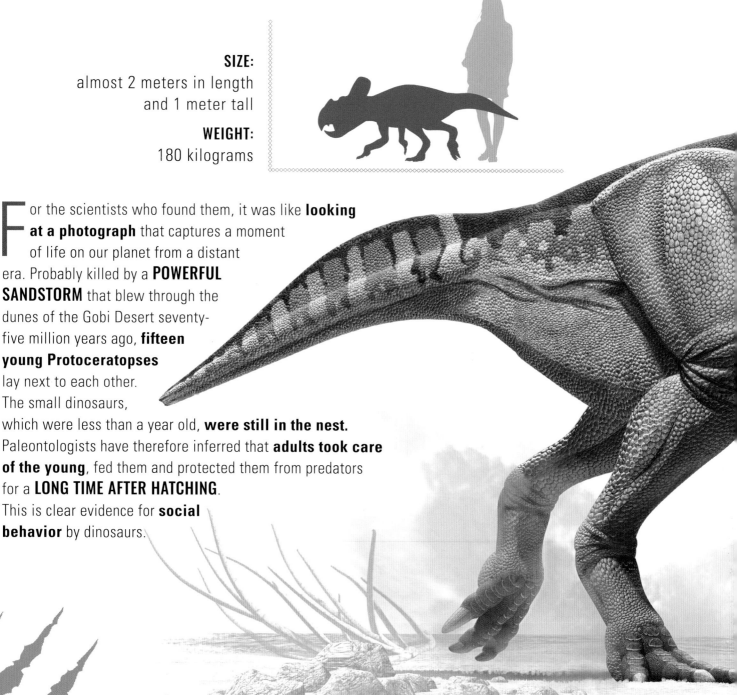

Protoceratopses were not very big: they were the **size of a calf**. They were herbivores and **FED ON LEATHERY PLANTS** that they broke into pieces with their hard beaks. They probably lived in herds and had a **big collar at the base of their head that may have been colorful** and could have served both to attract the attention of females during the mating period and to protect themselves from predators. They were, in fact, a **coveted prey for carnivores**, but they were difficult to overpower as they were able to defend themselves vehemently, as shown by some extraordinary fossils that have been discovered.

A FOSSIL FOUND IN THE GOBI DESERT IN MONGOLIA, WHICH HAS BECOME VERY FAMOUS, SHOWS A VELOCIRAPTOR CLUTCHED IN A DEATH GRIP WITH A PROTOCERATOPS. THE CARNIVORE, AFTER HAVING GRABBED ITS HEAD, PLUNGED A CLAW INTO THE THROAT OF THE PROTOCERATOPS, WHICH IN TURN WAS CLUTCHING THE RIGHT LEG OF THE PREDATOR IN ITS POWERFUL BEAK. THE TWO DIED AS THEY STRUGGLED AND WERE PRESERVED FOR MILLIONS OF YEARS, PASSING ON THIS FINAL BLOODY SCENE OF A PREHISTORIC DRAMA.

PARASAUROLOPHUS

WHERE IT LIVED:
North America

WHERE THE MOST IMPORTANT FOSSILS WERE FOUND:
Alberta (Canada), Utah and New Mexico (USA)

WHEN IT LIVED:
100 to 65 million years ago

SIZE:
up to 10 meters in length
and from 3 to 4.5 meters tall

WEIGHT:
from 2 to 3 tons

Some have called this dinosaur the **"GREAT TRUMPETER."** Why? It was able to emit incredible sounds. Its crest, over a meter long, was hollow and the maze of spaces inside it was connected to breathing: they were needed for the passage of air from the nostrils to the lungs. If necessary, however, Parasaurolophus used them as a **POWERFUL SOUNDING BOARD** to create sounds.

Two scholars have even managed to replicate these sounds. Using one of the **most complete fossil skulls** belonging to this species, that found near Farmington, New Mexico, they took 350 scans of the crest and **SIMULATED THE NOISE** that this animal could have produced with a sophisticated computer. The call that was produced was similar to that of **A GIANT WHO CLEARS HIS THROAT**.

Some scholars, when they heard it, have speculated that this distinctive trait served the purpose of allowing members of the same species to recognize each other at a considerable distance and even in the tangle of a dense forest.

These sounds were probably used by males to attract females and to **DEMONSTRATE THEIR POWER TO RIVALS**, thus avoiding violent physical clashes.

THE CREST OF PARASAUROLOPHUS WAS FOR A LONG TIME A MYSTERY. MANY HYPOTHESES WERE GIVEN TO EXPLAIN ITS FUNCTION BEFORE UNDERSTANDING THAT IT WAS USED TO PRODUCE SOUNDS. ONE OF THESE HYPOTHESES ARGUED THAT IT WAS A KIND OF BREATHING TUBE TO BE USED WHEN THE ANIMAL'S HEAD WAS COMPLETELY IMMERSED IN WATER LOOKING FOR AQUATIC PLANTS THAT IT THEN ATE.

ARGENTINOSAURUS

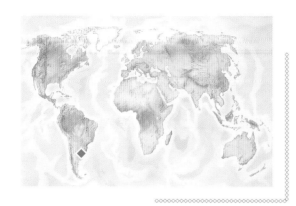

WHERE IT LIVED:
South America

WHERE THE MOST IMPORTANT FOSSILS WERE FOUND:
Argentina

WHEN IT LIVED:
95 million years ago

SIZE:
up to 30 meters in length
and up to 20 meters tall

WEIGHT:
over 80 tons

I t is probably the largest dinosaur that has ever been discovered. **ITS DIMENSIONS WERE ASTOUNDING**. It weighed as much as twenty elephants and one of its vertebrae was about the same size as an adult woman. **Its eggs seemed to be rugby balls**. In Patagonia, hundreds of these eggs were found, some of which still retained the fossilized imprint of the embryo's skin.
It is estimated that a small Argentinosaurus **took more than thirty years to reach the size of adult**, growing from a birth weight of 5 kilograms to reach 80 tons.

Argentinosaurus moved in herds that were not very large and fed mostly on coniferous trees that were ground up in its stomach using **stones that were ingested for this purpose** (known as **GASTROLITHS**). **The only predators that it feared was Giganotosaurus**, a carnivore that could reach up to 14 meters in length, and which attacked young or sick dinosaurs in groups of a dozen individuals. The outcome was not to be taken for granted and sometimes the assailant was the one that ended the fight badly.

ACCORDING TO SCHOLARS, THESE DINOSAURS (WHICH BELONGED TO A GROUP OF SAUROPODS CALLED TITANOSAURS) EVOLVED TO BECOME THIS SIZE FOR TWO REASONS. GIANT ANIMALS OF THIS SIZE NOT ONLY HAD A BETTER CHANCE OF SURVIVING THE PREDATORS THAT ATTACKED THEM MORE INFREQUENTLY AS THEY WERE DISCOURAGED BY THEIR SIZE, BUT THEY COULD EVEN REACH FOOD AT HEIGHTS WHICH OTHER HERBIVOROUS DINOSAURS COULD NOT, LIKE THAT FOUND AT THE TOP OF THE BIG CONIFEROUS TREES.

NODOSAURUS

WHERE IT LIVED:
North America

WHERE THE MOST IMPORTANT FOSSILS WERE FOUND:
Wyoming, Kansas (USA)

WHEN IT LIVED:
95 to 90 million years ago

SIZE:
up to 6 meters in length
and up to 2 meters tall

WEIGHT:
up to 1 ton

NODOSAURUS was one of the **first armored dinosaurs** to have been discovered. Its fossil remains were unearthed in 1889 in the US state of Wyoming. Since then, paleontologists have found very little other evidence, therefore what is known of this dinosaur is still quite uncertain and based on **very incomplete specimens**. It is thought, however, that this herbivore had a **RELATIVELY SMALL HEAD** compared to the rest of its body which was covered with **bony plates and full of knots and bumps** (its name actually means **"KNOTTED LIZARD"**). When it was in danger, it reacted a bit **like armadillos** do: it flattened itself to the ground to protect its **stomach that was not "armored"** like its back and curled up as much as possible becoming an **impregnable fortress**. At this point, the predator, attacking with its teeth, could not hurt it: a **PASSIVE DEFENSE TECHNIQUE** but a **very effective** one. On the other hand, it did not have many other defense options if its short, stubby legs that made it move slowly and clumsily are considered.

ONE OF THE UNANSWERED QUESTIONS ABOUT NODOSAURUS IS WHETHER OR NOT IT HAD A ROW
OF SHARP SPIKES ON EACH OF ITS SIDES. OTHER DINOSAURS BELONGING TO THE SAME FAMILY OF NODOSAURIDAE,
SUCH AS THE POLACANTHUS OR THE HYLAEOSAURUS, WERE EQUIPPED WITH THEM. THE SPIKES WOULD HAVE MADE
ITS ABILITY TO DEFEND ITSELF FROM PREDATORS MUCH MORE EFFECTIVE, AS IT COULD HAVE STRUCK CARNIVORES
AS THEY WERE ATTACKING, INFLICTING SERIOUS INJURIES.

STYRACOSAURUS

WHERE IT LIVED:
North America

WHERE THE MOST IMPORTANT FOSSILS WERE FOUND:
Arizona (USA), Alberta (Canada)

WHEN IT LIVED:
80 to 75 million years ago

SIZE:
up to 5.5 meters in length
and up to 2.5 meters tall

WEIGHT:
3 tons

Styracosaurus means **"lizard with spikes"** and there could not have been a better name: its appearance was really strange! It had a **LARGE HORN ON ITS NOSE**, up to one meter in length, and a **GIANT CREST** behind its skull with at least **six long, enormous, spiky bumps**. What they were used for remains a mystery. Initially it was thought that they were used to defend it against predators, but today, another hypothesis has been put forward: the bumps could possibly have been **a sign of distinction** that allowed different individuals to recognize one another from a distance.

ven the **large collar bone** surely had an important function. It was first of all a **defensive element** against enemics; in addition, regulating the flow of the blood in this area **changed the color of the skin that it covered**, signaling the availability of the males to the females and discouraging potential love rivals. Fossil findings have allowed paleontologists to speculate that these **ENORMOUS HERBIVOROUS DINOSAURS** often gathered in herds composed of numerous individuals. Because "unity is strength", this was a **defense strategy** against voracious carnivores like the giant Daspletosaurus, which towered at up to 9 meters tall, and which like Styracosaurus, wandered the area of North America during the same period.

DESCRIBED AS "BONE BEDS", LARGE DEPOSITS OF STYRACOSAURUS FOSSILS HAVE BEEN FOUND IN ALBERTA, CANADA. THEIR DISCOVERY LED TO THE HYPOTHESIS THAT THESE DINOSAURS MOVED IN HERDS. THESE PARTICULAR STYRACOSAURUS, PERHAPS IN AN ATTEMPT TO CROSS A BODY OF WATER, WERE SURPRISED BY A FLOOD. SWEPT AWAY BY THE CURRENT, THEY ALL DROWNED AND WERE DRAGGED TO THE PLACE WHERE THEIR FOSSIL REMAINS HAVE BEEN FOUND.

MAIASAURA

WHERE IT LIVED:
North America

WHERE THE MOST IMPORTANT FOSSILS WERE FOUND:
Montana (USA)

WHEN IT LIVED:
76 million years ago

SIZE:
up to 9 meters in length
and over 2 meters tall

WEIGHT:
up to 3 tons

I n the summer of 1978, American paleontologists **Jack Horner and Bob Makela** made an incredible discovery that would forever change our understanding of dinosaurs. After having found the remains of **A CONICAL-SHAPED MUD NEST** in Montana which contained the bodies of fifteen fossilized baby dinosaurs, they realized that these babies had remained in the nest for a long period of time after hatching. They had skeletons that were relatively developed and had therefore been **born a few months before**. Their teeth showed signs of wear due to the chewing of food, while **many fragments of eggshells** recovered in the nest had been crushed by the trampling of their legs. After weeks of digging, paleontologists had found **HUNDREDS OF EGGS** and dozens of dinosaur skeletons of different ages still in the nests (which were no more than 7 or 8 meters from each other), while others were scattered in the surrounding area. This certainly provides evidence that these animals were **LIVING IN A GROUP, LOOKING AFTER THE NESTS** and continuing to take care of the small dinosaurs for a long period after hatching. It was the nesting area of a new species of dinosaur which they named **MAIASAURA ("GOOD MOTHER LIZARD")** to highlight the most important characteristic of this dinosaur that took care of their offspring: a behavior which no one had hypothesized for dinosaurs up to this point.

THE FACT THAT THE FOSSIL SKELETONS OF THE BABY MAIASAURA FOUND IN THE NESTS HAD DIFFERENT AGES (SOME MEASURED JUST HALF A METER WHILE OTHERS WERE ALMOST TWO METERS LONG) SUGGESTS THAT THE MOTHER DINOSAUR WENT TO FIND FOOD FOR THEM. SHE THEN RETURNED WITH BERRIES AND VEGETABLES THAT SHE PROBABLY REGURGITATED INTO THE NEST SO THAT THE YOUNG DINOSAURS COULD FEED THEMSELVES.

PACHYCEPHALOSAURUS

WHERE IT LIVED:
North America

WHERE THE MOST IMPORTANT FOSSILS WERE FOUND:
Wyoming, Montana, South Dakota (USA)

WHEN IT LIVED:
76 to 65 million years ago

SIZE:
more than 4 meters in length
and up to 2 meters tall

WEIGHT:
450 kilograms

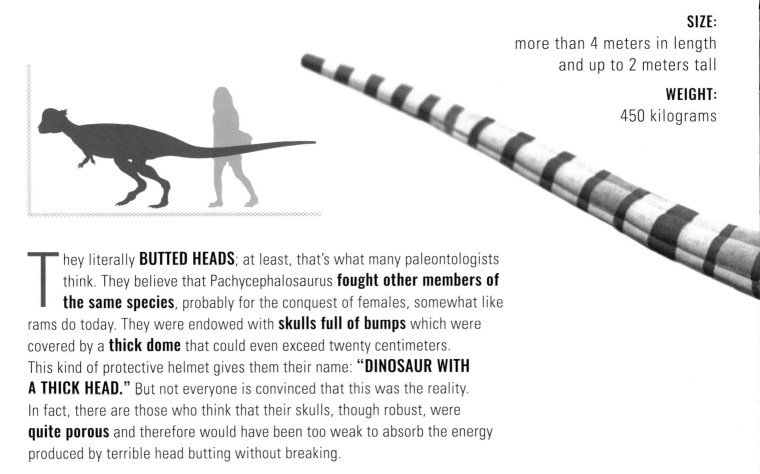

They literally **BUTTED HEADS**; at least, that's what many paleontologists think. They believe that Pachycephalosaurus **fought other members of the same species**, probably for the conquest of females, somewhat like rams do today. They were endowed with **skulls full of bumps** which were covered by a **thick dome** that could even exceed twenty centimeters. This kind of protective helmet gives them their name: **"DINOSAUR WITH A THICK HEAD."** But not everyone is convinced that this was the reality. In fact, there are those who think that their skulls, though robust, were **quite porous** and therefore would have been too weak to absorb the energy produced by terrible head butting without breaking.

Unfortunately, only **a few fossils have been found** of this dinosaur. According to the reconstructions made based on what has been found thus far, we know that Pachycephalosaurus moved on its two hind legs, but that it **was not very fast**. It was equipped with **SMALL, SHARP TEETH**, and was mostly herbivorous though its diet could be rounded out with **seeds, fruits and insects**.

IN 2012, AMERICAN PALEONTOLOGIST **JOSEPH PETERSON** MADE A CT SCAN OF A PACHYCEPHALOSAURUS SKULL AND FOUND SEVERAL SIGNS OF TRAUMA ON THE THICKEST PART OF THE SKULL: THIS KIND OF WOUND WOULD BE EXPECTED FROM FIGHTING HEAD TO HEAD. HE THEN SOUGHT OTHER EVIDENCE, WITHOUT FINDING ANY, ON THE SKULLS OF FEMALES AND YOUNG PACHYCEPHALOSAURUS. IT COULD BE THEREFORE CONFIRMED THAT ONLY THE MALES FOUGHT EACH OTHER.

TARCHIA

WHERE IT LIVED:
Mongolia

WHERE THE MOST IMPORTANT FOSSILS WERE FOUND:
Gobi Desert (Mongolia)

WHEN IT LIVED:
72 million years ago

SIZE:
up to 8.5 meters in length
and up to 2 meters tall

WEIGHT:
almost 4 tons

S eeing it approach must have been an impressive sight. It was a **giant beast over eight meters long**, weighing nearly as much as a bus, covered with armor and **full of sharp spikes**, which made the ground tremble every time it took a step. Tarchia is certainly one of the most astonishing **ARMORED DINOSAURS**.

t was even feared by large carnivores like Tarbosaurus, which roamed during the same time period in search of prey in the **present Gobi Desert** in Mongolia, where its fossils were found. However, despite being a **WAR MACHINE IN MOTION**, its name highlights another aspect of this dinosaur.
In Mongolian, Tarchia means **"WITH A BRAIN."** It had a **skull** about 40 cm in length and nearly the same in width, **larger than that of other Ankylosauridae** (the dinosaur family to which it belonged).
The paleontologists who named it were especially struck by the fact that it was **much larger than that of Saichania**, a dinosaur that was similar to it but larger in size, which was found in the same place where the remains of Tarchia were found.

THE VERTEBRAE OF ITS TAIL, WHICH WAS ARMED WITH A BONE CLUB AT THE END, WERE FUSED TOGETHER IN ORDER TO MAKE IT RIGID. THIS WAY, TARCHIA COULD USE IT AS A DEADLY CLUB, ABLE TO INFLICT DEEP WOUNDS ON OR EVEN KILL THE LARGEST PREDATORS.

ANKYLOSAURUS

WHERE IT LIVED:
North America

WHERE THE MOST IMPORTANT FOSSILS WERE FOUND:
Wyoming, Montana (USA), Alberta (Canada)

WHEN IT LIVED:
70 to 66 million years ago

SIZE:
more than 6 meters in length
and almost 2 meters tall

WEIGHT:
up to 6 tons

Thanks to its **ARMOR**, consisting of **hundreds of external bony plates stuck together**, Ankylosaurus was a true **fortress in motion**. It also possessed a weapon capable of doing real damage.

Its tail, rugged and packed with strong muscles, had a **BONY BUMP** on the final part, which it turned into a **club** capable of inflicting deadly blows to his enemies.

Some of the fossils of **TAIL CLUBS** from Ankylosaurus show signs of damage as if they had struck something hard. Nevertheless, these dinosaurs often fell **victim to T-Rex**, with its extraordinary bite that **was able to perforate the armor**. But predators aside, the life of an Ankylosaurus was spent relatively calmly. It **moved slowly**, leading a **SOLITARY EXISTENCE** in what is now North America, in search of food which consisted of low plants which it tore up and ate with its beak-shaped mouth.

ANOTHER STRATEGY THAT ANKLYOSAURUS PROBABLY ADOPTED TO DEFEND ITSELF AGAINST ITS ENEMIES WAS TO CROUCH DOWN UNDER ITS ARMOR, FLATTENING ITS STOMACH ON THE GROUND TO PROTECT THE SOFT UNDERBELLY THAT WAS THE MOST VULNERABLE PART OF HIS BODY.

STYGIMOLOCH

WHERE IT LIVED:
North America

WHERE THE MOST IMPORTANT FOSSILS WERE FOUND:
Wyoming, Montana (USA)

WHEN IT LIVED:
70 to 66 million years ago

SIZE:
up to 3 meters in length
and up to 1.5 meters tall

WEIGHT:
up to 90 kilograms

When the fossilized remains of a dinosaur are first unearthed, paleontologists try to figure out **what the dinosaur would have looked like** alive. They try to reconstruct the skeleton and check if it comes from a species that has already been discovered in the past or whether it is something new. In the latter case, the dinosaur is given a name. But sometimes, paleontologists make mistakes. This is what happened in the case of Stygimoloch. Some fossils were found at the end of the nineteenth century, but it was only after subsequent discoveries in 1982 that paleontologists were able to describe it fully. It was originally thought to have been a **NEW SPECIES OF HERBIVOROUS DINOSAUR** from Pachycephalosaurus family, with which it shared similar **bumps on its head**, although it was smaller and its skull was not as thick.

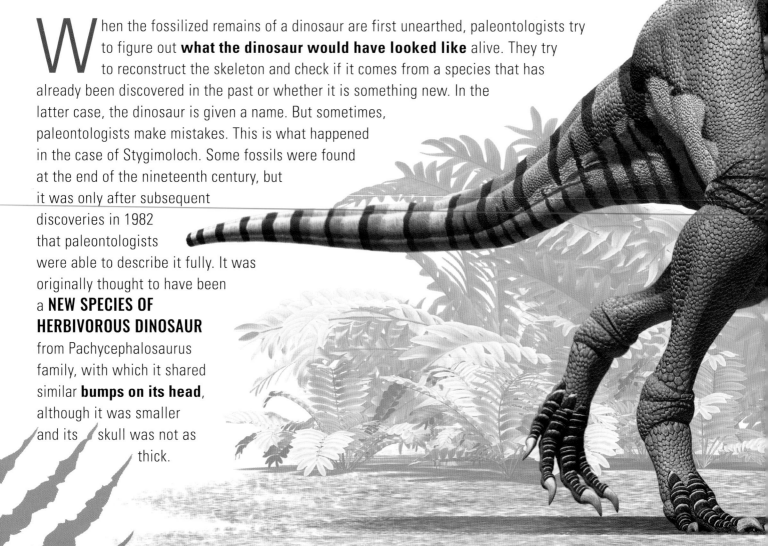

Therefore, because of its appearance, they called this dinosaur the **"DEMON OF THE RIVER STYX"** (Stygimoloch). In recent years, however, doubts have arisen. Some paleontologists believe that this dinosaur does not belong to a separate species but that it is actually a Pachycephalosaurus in its **juvenile form**. How could such a mistake have been made? There are a few possible answers. First of all, it is possible for animals to have different aspects from their adult form in various phases of growth, and secondly, **the males and females of the same species sometimes have different physical characteristics**. When there are only a few examples of their remains, it is difficult to detect these differences immediately. According to some studies, of all the species that were considered new during discoveries made between 1850 and 1980, almost half of them should be **CONSIDERED ERRORS** and they can actually be traced to existing species. Fortunately, with time, more detailed research allow us to **"rewrite" and correct** the pages of the great, extraordinary book of prehistory.

IN 2004, IN SOUTH DAKOTA, A SKULL FULL OF SPIKY BUMPS WAS DISCOVERED. IT WAS THOUGHT TO BE A NEW SPECIES AND ITS REALLY BIZARRE APPEARANCE LED TO IT BEING CALLED "DRACOREX HOGWARTSIA", WHICH MEANS "DRAGON KING OF HOGWARTS" ("HOGWARTS" IS THE MAGIC SCHOOL IN THE HARRY POTTER BOOK SERIES). TODAY, HOWEVER, SOME RESEARCHERS THINK THAT DRACOREX, JUST AS STYGIMOLOCH, IS NOT A SEPARATE SPECIES, BUT RATHER AN IMMATURE EXAMPLE OF A PACHYCEPHALOSAURUS THAT DURING THE COURSE OF GROWTH WOULD HAVE CHANGED ITS FEATURES TO THE POINT THAT THE THICK DOME THAT CHARACTERIZED THE SKULL OF ADULTS WOULD HAVE APPEARED.

TRICERATOPS

WHERE IT LIVED:
North America

WHERE THE MOST IMPORTANT FOSSILS WERE FOUND:
United States of America, Canada

WHEN IT LIVED:
67 to 65 million years ago

SIZE:
from 7 to 9 meters in length
and 3 meters tall

PESO:
from 6 to 9 tons

When the first **TWO HUGE HORN FOSSILS** were discovered in 1887 in Denver, Colorado, they were thought to have belonged to a **giant bison that was now extinct.** No one ever imagined that shortly thereafter the remains of this animal would pop up bit by bit all over the place. It was a **large dinosaur.** Since then, hundreds of Triceratops fossils have been found, all belonging, according to scholars, to two main species, **TRICERATOPS HORRIDUS** and **TRICERATOPS PRORSUS.**

TRICERATOPS roamed our planet at the end of the **Cretaceous Period** in what is now known as North America. Because of their size, they **moved relatively slowly**: according to some estimates, they reached a top speed of **8 km/h** (in comparison, the fearsome Velociraptor could reach up to 60 km/h!). They were **herbivores** and spent most of their day **feeding on low plants**.

Their mouth, in the **SHAPE OF A BEAK** similar to that of parrots but much larger, was filled with **hundreds of thin, sharp teeth**, able to grind up even the toughest plants and which were arranged in several columns, each composed of **3-5 teeth one above the other**: when a tooth had been used up, there was already one ready underneath that replaced it.

According to scholars, they **moved in great herds**, like other species of herbivorous dinosaurs, but also in **SMALL FAMILIES**, such as that discovered in 2012 by paleontologist Peter Larson, who unearthed the remains of **three Triceratops of different sizes**. There were probably **TWO ADULTS WITH A CUB** that had been surprised and attacked by a Tyrannosaurus Rex. The remains of the largest specimen, in fact, show the signs of bites from that terrible carnivore.

TRICERATOPS

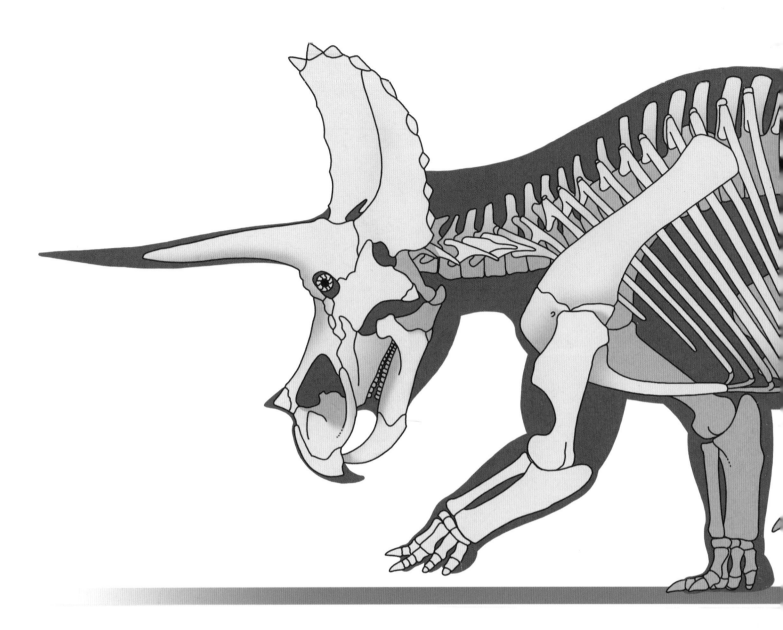

The most amazing thing about these dinosaurs was definitely **THEIR HEAD**, with a skull that could measure up to **TWO METERS**, a **large collar bone and three horns** that gave them their name (**TRICERATOPS** in ancient Greek means **"THREE-HORNED FACE"**). The males used them to defend themselves from predators and to protect their young (when there was some kind of **danger**, a group of adult Triceratops probably **formed a circle**, putting the cubs in the center, so that they formed an impenetrable wall, **just as bison and musk oxen do today**). **The horns** were also used in **duels between males** for the conquest of females. The fights were often violent, as demonstrated by the serious wounds inflicted on the contenders evidenced in the fossils.

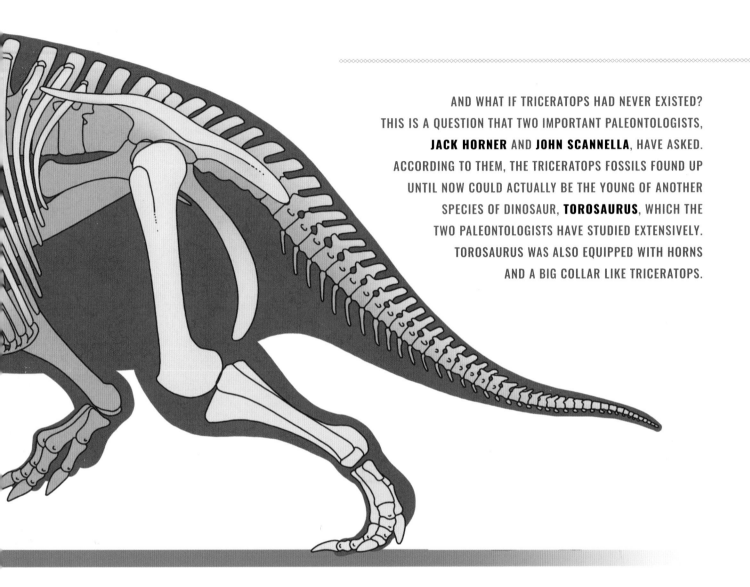

AND WHAT IF TRICERATOPS HAD NEVER EXISTED?
THIS IS A QUESTION THAT TWO IMPORTANT PALEONTOLOGISTS,
JACK HORNER AND **JOHN SCANNELLA**, HAVE ASKED.
ACCORDING TO THEM, THE TRICERATOPS FOSSILS FOUND UP
UNTIL NOW COULD ACTUALLY BE THE YOUNG OF ANOTHER
SPECIES OF DINOSAUR, **TOROSAURUS**, WHICH THE
TWO PALEONTOLOGISTS HAVE STUDIED EXTENSIVELY.
TOROSAURUS WAS ALSO EQUIPPED WITH HORNS
AND A BIG COLLAR LIKE TRICERATOPS.

BUT IF TOROSAURUS WAS ACTUALLY THE ADULT FORM OF TRICERATOPS,
WHY ARE TOROSAURUS FOSSILS RARER THAN THOSE OF TRICERATOPS?
MAYBE THE NUMBER OF YOUNG DINOSAURS WAS GREATER THAN THAT OF ADULTS.
THE MORTALITY RATE WAS HIGH AND MANY DID NOT SURVIVE TO MATURITY.
HOWEVER, THE ANSWER COULD ALSO BE ANOTHER: SOME SCIENTISTS ARGUE
THAT TOROSAURUS WAS SIMPLY THE MALE OR FEMALE
VERSION OF TRICERATOPS.

THE LARGE AQUATIC REPTILES FROM THE TIME OF THE DINOSAURS

THE TERROR OF THE SEAS

ABOUT 250 MILLION YEARS AGO, THE LAND THAT RAISED UP WAS JOINED TOGETHER IN ONE CONTINENTAL MASS KNOWN AS THE **PANGEA**, AND EVERYTHING ELSE WAS WATER. THESE WATERS WERE A HABITAT THAT SOON CALLED TO MANY REPTILES THAT HAD EVOLVED ON THE MAINLAND AND AT THAT POINT WERE **IN THE BEST CONDITIONS TO RETURN TO THE SEAS**, WHERE THERE WAS LESS COMPETITION FOR FOOD. THE OCEANS OF THE JURASSIC PERIOD SAW THESE ANIMALS LIVE, REPRODUCE, AND DIVERSIFY INTO MANY FORMS TO BECOME THE RULERS OF THE WATERS OF THE PLANET. WHEN **FOSSIL HUNTERS** BEGAN TO BRING TO LIGHT THEIR REMAINS IN THE NINETEENTH CENTURY, WHAT THEY FOUND WAS SO UNUSUAL THAT IT WAS HARD TO BELIEVE THAT IT COULD BE TRUE.

SINCE THEN, HUNDREDS OF SPECIES AND DIFFERENT KINDS OF **AQUATIC REPTILES** HAVE BEEN FOUND. SOME FOSSILS ARE SO UNBELIEVABLE THAT THEY SEEM TO BE **TRUE "PHOTOGRAPHS" IMPRINTED ON THE ROCKS**. BY STUDYING AND ANALYZING THEM, PALEONTOLOGISTS HAVE RECONSTRUCTED THE APPEARANCE, HABITS AND BEHAVIOR OF THESE ANIMALS. THEY TELL THE EXTRAORDINARY STORIES OF THESE ANIMALS THAT WOULD

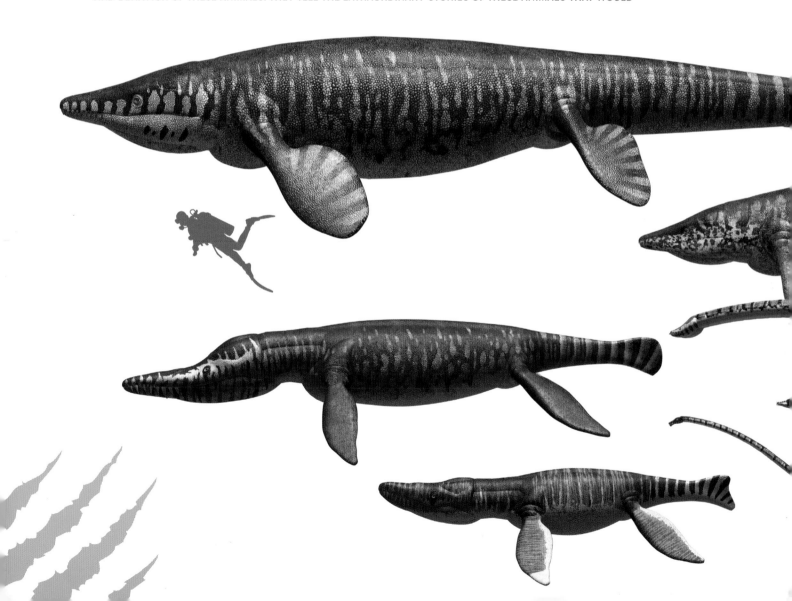

OTHERWISE BE LOST IN THE FOLDS OF TIME. TODAY WE KNOW THAT THE **SIZE** OF AQUATIC REPTILES COULD VARY FROM **THAT OF A DOLPHIN TO THAT OF A HUGE WHALE**. THEY WERE ALMOST ALWAYS EFFICIENT PREDATORS AND SOME WERE REALLY TERRIFYING. AN EXAMPLE OF THESE WAS THE **TILOSAURUS** THAT WITH ITS BIG JAWS WAS THE EQUIVALENT OF A T-REX IN THE OCEANS. THE **MOSASAURUS** SHOULD ALSO BE MENTIONED AS IT COULD REACH UP TO 14 METERS IN LENGTH. IT WAS SO AGGRESSIVE THAT EVEN MEMBERS OF ITS OWN SPECIES OFTEN ENDED UP IN ITS STOMACH.

BUT EVEN IF THESE EXAMPLES WERE PROBABLY **SOLITARY HUNTERS, OTHER AQUATIC REPTILES PROBABLY LIVED IN AND MOVED AROUND IN HERDS**. IN NEVADA, UNITED STATES, DOZENS OF **SHONISAURUS** SKELETONS WERE FOSSILIZED ALL IN THE SAME DIRECTION AS IF THEIR DEATH HAD OCCURRED WHILE THEY WERE GATHERED SWIMMING IN A GROUP. SOME SPECIES MAY HAVE **GONE ONTO LAND TO LAY THEIR EGGS**, WHILE **OTHERS GATHERED SEASONALLY IN COASTAL WATERS** THAT WERE CALMER AND MORE PROTECTED FROM PREDATORS, WHERE THEY RETURNED TO DELIVER THEIR YOUNG.

SOME FINDINGS HAVE EVEN REVEALED SCENES OF DAILY LIFE, THAT HELP US TO UNDERSTAND HOW THOSE EXTRAORDINARY CREATURES LIVED BEFORE SOMETHING DISTURBED THEIR WORLD AND AS THE DINOSAURS THEY **DISAPPEARED FOREVER BECOMING EXTINCT**.

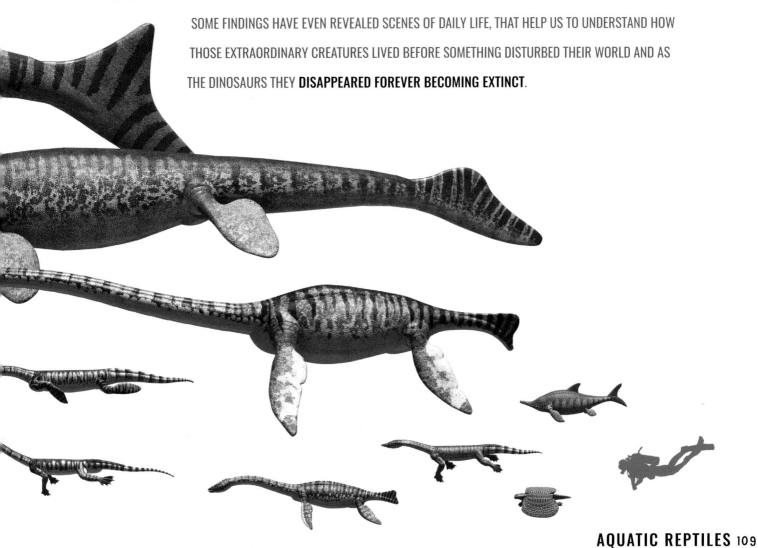

CERESIOSAURUS

WHERE IT LIVED:
Italy, Switzerland

WHERE THE MOST IMPORTANT FOSSILS WERE FOUND:
Monte San Giorgio (Italy)

WHEN IT LIVED:
240 million years ago

SIZE:
up to 4 meters in length

WEIGHT:
200 to 300 kilograms

One of the best known fossils of this species is truly unique: on the same slab of rock, seven small skeletons of Neusticosaurus and a large example of a Ceresiosaurus are found together. It looks like a peaceful "snapshot" from the distant past, but it is instead the remains of a prehistoric drama, probably **a hunting scene**. **CERESIOSAURUS** was the predator and those little Neusticosaurus would have been its prey. They were found in **Monte San Giorgio** (on the border between Italy and Switzerland) which at that time, about 240 million years ago, was not yet a mountain, but the **seabed of a shallow sea**.

There would have been islets and sandbars that separated the coast from the open waters and would have created **a large coastal lagoon**, a landscape that would have been similar to that of the Bahamas or the Maldives today. This was the habitat where Ceresiosaurus lived and hunted. On the day that it ended becoming a fossil, something did not go the right way and the killer and its victims died together. **Their bodies ended up on the seabed**, where they were covered with mud. The rest was taken care of by time: over millennia, their bones were transformed into **FOSSILS** which scholars then rediscovered.

THIS HUGE LIZARD SWAM QUICKLY IN SEARCH OF ITS PREY, GRABBING IT WITH SHARP TEETH. ITS HIND LEGS, LONGER AND MORE POWERFUL THAN THE FRONT ONES, GAVE IT GREATER THRUST DURING THE HUNT. THE FAVORITE VICTIMS OF CERESIOSAURUS WERE OTHER AQUATIC REPTILES OR SMALL FISH.

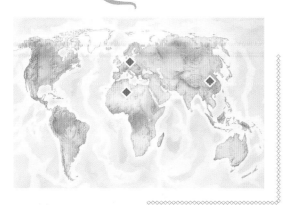

NOTHOSAURUS

WHERE IT LIVED:
North Africa, Europe, China

WHERE THE MOST IMPORTANT FOSSILS WERE FOUND:
Germany

WHEN IT LIVED:
240 million years ago

SIZE:
up to 4 meters in length

WEIGHT:
from 20 to 100 kilograms

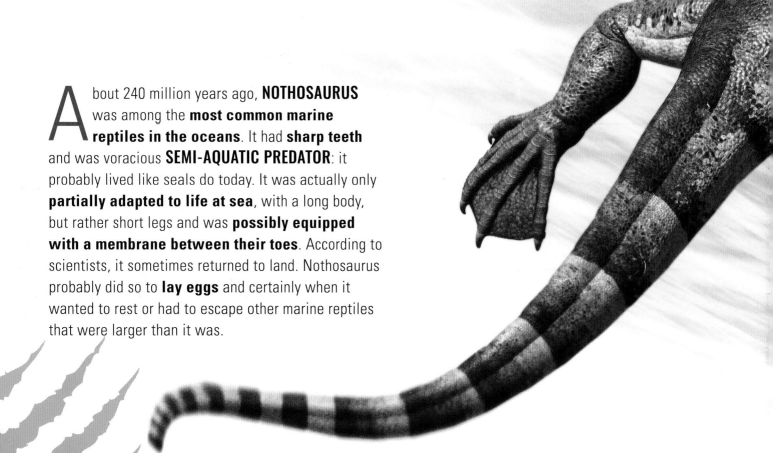

About 240 million years ago, **NOTHOSAURUS** was among the **most common marine reptiles in the oceans**. It had **sharp teeth** and was voracious **SEMI-AQUATIC PREDATOR**: it probably lived like seals do today. It was actually only **partially adapted to life at sea**, with a long body, but rather short legs and was **possibly equipped with a membrane between their toes**. According to scientists, it sometimes returned to land. Nothosaurus probably did so to **lay eggs** and certainly when it wanted to rest or had to escape other marine reptiles that were larger than it was.

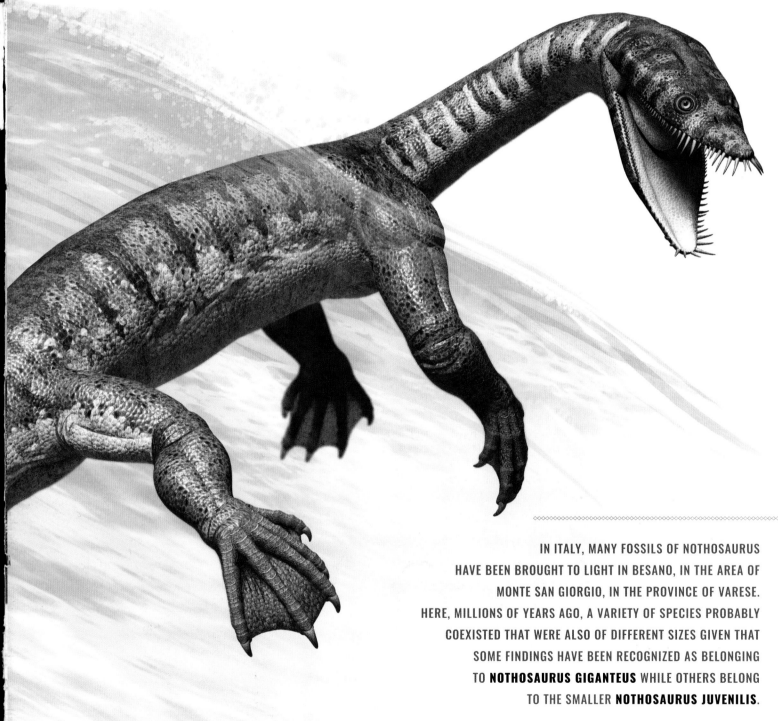

t was not clear how Nothosaurus swam, until the discovery in China in 2014, of **a number of fossilized footprints** on an ancient path on the seabed. The tracks are **ARRANGED IN PAIRS**, in long series of ten or fifteen. The size and the space between the tracks suggest that they were left by the front legs of these animals and they demonstrate that they **swam by moving their limbs in unison downwardly** like paddles (instead of laterally as penguins do today, for example).

IN ITALY, MANY FOSSILS OF NOTHOSAURUS HAVE BEEN BROUGHT TO LIGHT IN BESANO, IN THE AREA OF MONTE SAN GIORGIO, IN THE PROVINCE OF VARESE. HERE, MILLIONS OF YEARS AGO, A VARIETY OF SPECIES PROBABLY COEXISTED THAT WERE ALSO OF DIFFERENT SIZES GIVEN THAT SOME FINDINGS HAVE BEEN RECOGNIZED AS BELONGING TO **NOTHOSAURUS GIGANTEUS** WHILE OTHERS BELONG TO THE SMALLER **NOTHOSAURUS JUVENILIS**.

TANYSTROPHEUS

WHERE IT LIVED:
Italy, Switzerland (German part)

WHERE THE MOST IMPORTANT FOSSILS WERE FOUND:
Besano (Italy)

WHEN IT LIVED:
230 million years ago

SIZE:
up to 6 meters in length

WEIGHT:
up to 200 kilograms

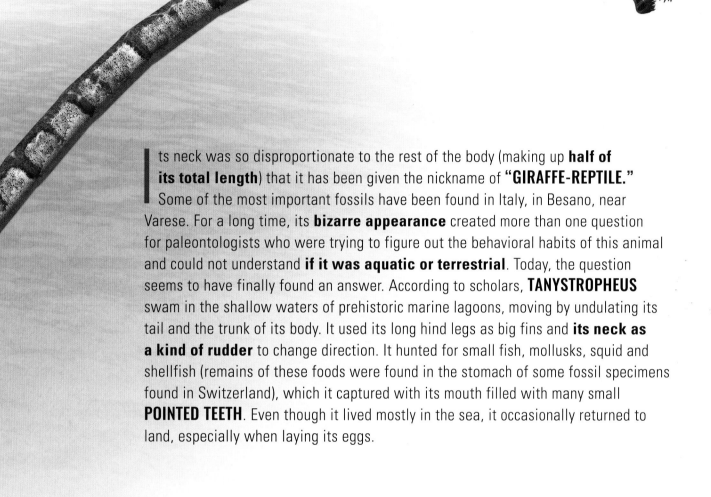

ts neck was so disproportionate to the rest of the body (making up **half of its total length**) that it has been given the nickname of **"GIRAFFE-REPTILE."** Some of the most important fossils have been found in Italy, in Besano, near Varese. For a long time, its **bizarre appearance** created more than one question for paleontologists who were trying to figure out the behavioral habits of this animal and could not understand **if it was aquatic or terrestrial**. Today, the question seems to have finally found an answer. According to scholars, **TANYSTROPHEUS** swam in the shallow waters of prehistoric marine lagoons, moving by undulating its tail and the trunk of its body. It used its long hind legs as big fins and **its neck as a kind of rudder** to change direction. It hunted for small fish, mollusks, squid and shellfish (remains of these foods were found in the stomach of some fossil specimens found in Switzerland), which it captured with its mouth filled with many small **POINTED TEETH**. Even though it lived mostly in the sea, it occasionally returned to land, especially when laying its eggs.

AT THE BEGINNING OF THE TWENTIETH CENTURY, SCHOLARS WHO ANALYZED THE FIRST FOSSILS OF TANYSTROPHEUS MISTOOK IT FOR A FLYING REPTILE. WHAT CONFUSED THEM WAS THE PRESENCE OF LONG BONES THAT LOOKED LIKE THE PHALANGES OF A FINGER SIMILAR TO A PATAGIUM (I.E. THE MEMBRANE FOUND IN WINGS) OF SOME PREHISTORIC ANIMALS THAT COULD FLY. SUBSEQUENT FINDS CLARIFIED THAT THESE BONES WERE ACTUALLY THE VERTEBRAE OF ITS LONG, ASTONISHING NECK.

HENODUS

WHERE IT LIVED:
Europe

WHERE THE MOST IMPORTANT FOSSILS WERE FOUND:
Germany

WHEN IT LIVED:
225 million years ago

SIZE:
more than 1 meter in length

WEIGHT:
up to 150 kilograms

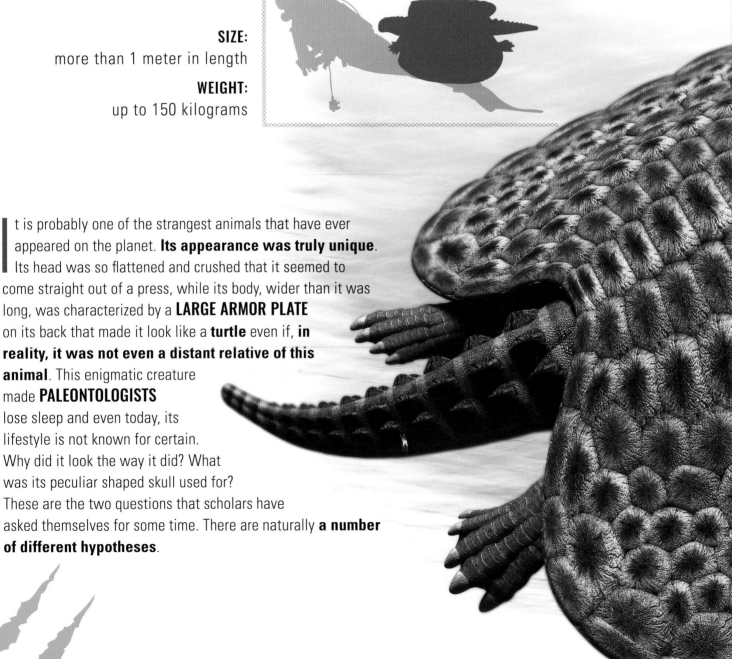

It is probably one of the strangest animals that have ever appeared on the planet. **Its appearance was truly unique**. Its head was so flattened and crushed that it seemed to come straight out of a press, while its body, wider than it was long, was characterized by a **LARGE ARMOR PLATE** on its back that made it look like a **turtle** even if, **in reality, it was not even a distant relative of this animal**. This enigmatic creature made **PALEONTOLOGISTS** lose sleep and even today, its lifestyle is not known for certain. Why did it look the way it did? What was its peculiar shaped skull used for? These are the two questions that scholars have asked themselves for some time. There are naturally **a number of different hypotheses**.

HENODUS probably spent its life in the quiet waters of coastal marshes, where its **strange flat jaw that was almost toothless** (it had **ONLY FOUR TEETH**) allowed it to sift the muddy bottom of the marsh to search for crustaceans which it ate. It is not out of the question that it had a **BALEEN-LIKE** structures in its mouth (similar to that of modern whales), which it used to filter the water and retain small prey.

It breathed air and had **a partly amphibious existence**. In fact, it often returned to land to rest and reproduce although its **ARMOR PLATE** made its movements on land rather awkward.

HENODUS' ARMOR PLATE WAS MADE FROM THE FUSION OF A LARGE NUMBER OF BONE PLATES. THEY FORMED A STURDY SHELL THAT PROTECTED IT FROM ITS ENEMIES, EVEN THOSE WITH THE MOST POWERFUL BITES. THIS DEFENSE STRATEGY HAD ONLY ONE WEAKNESS: UNLIKE TURTLES TODAY, HENODUS WAS NOT ABLE TO RETRACT ITS LEGS AND HEAD INSIDE THE ARMOR, LEAVING THEM EXPOSED AND VULNERABLE. GENERALLY, HOWEVER, IN THE HEAT OF AN ATTACK IN WATER, PREDATORS AIMED AT THE BIGGER TARGET, THE BODY, AND ONLY RARELY AT THE EXTREMITIES. THIS ALLOWED HENODUS TO SURVIVE IN MOST CASES.

PLESIOSAURUS

WHERE IT LIVED:
The Seas of Northern Europe

WHERE THE MOST IMPORTANT FOSSILS WERE FOUND:
Dorset (United Kingdom), Germany

WHEN IT LIVED:
205 to 65 million years ago

SIZE:
up to 5 meters in length
and 1.5 meters tall

WEIGHT:
from 500 kilograms to 2 tons

I t looked like a **"SEA DRAGON"** from legends in Medieval times. When the remains of this large animal were discovered in 1823, nobody had ever seen a creature like it, and the geologist and paleontologist William Conybeare described it as **"a snake that passes through a turtle shell**." They later chose the name **PLESIOSAURUS** for it, a name which means **"RELATED TO LIZARDS."**

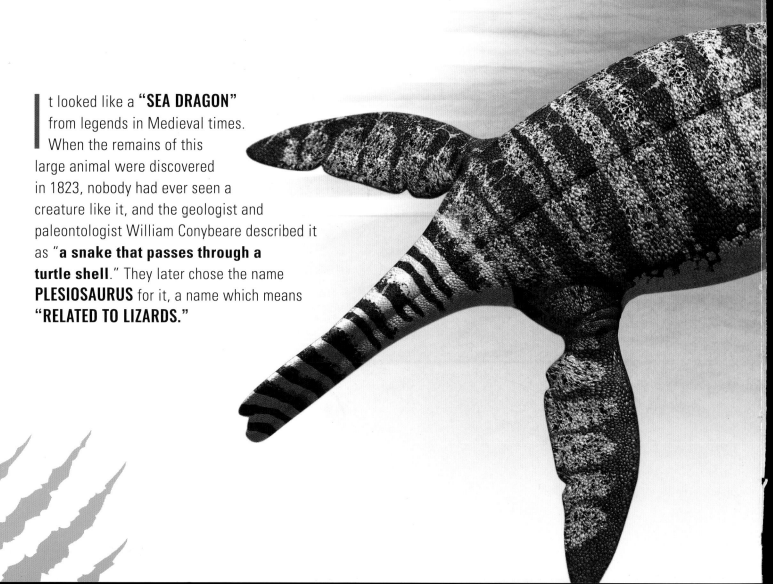

oday we know that it was a marine reptile from the Jurassic Period, but when the fossil was reconstructed in full, it was realized that it would not be easy to understand its behavior. For this reason, the **first hypotheses** on how it lived and its daily habits were quite **imaginative**. According to some scholars, they could "coil up" their neck like a snake, while others argued that they were able to walk on land. Over time, **scientists have put together a more accurate identikit** and these assumptions today almost make us smile. Plesiosaurus had **A SMALL HEAD**, a mouth filled with **SHARP TEETH** and four legs that over time had become **TRUE FINS** used to swim in a manner **similar to an underwater flight**.

PLESIOSAURUS

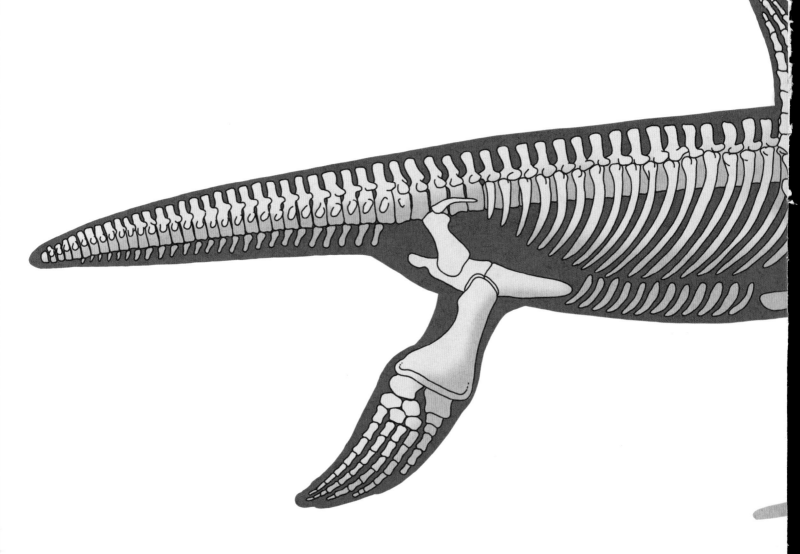

ts neck was long and slender and the animal used it to approach prey
without them noticing. **It fed on fish, cephalopods and other small
aquatic reptiles**. It is almost certain that, because of its long neck and
body size, it was **not able to move around on the sand**, even to lay eggs,
as some scholars have claimed. A surprising discovery made a few years
ago allowed scholars to discover that Plesiosaurus was **VIVIPAROUS**, that **it
gave birth to its young** and that it did it **IN THE WATER**, which was the its
habitat. A fossil, unearthed in Kansas (United States) in 1987, still had the
fetus in its belly. This **"PREHISTORIC MOTHER"** did not survive to give birth
and so the fetus died and was fossilized with her.

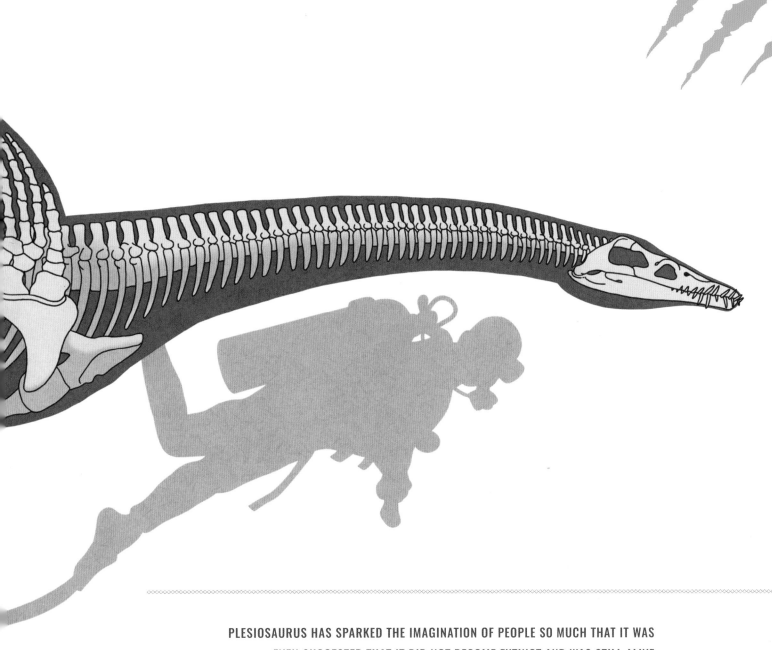

PLESIOSAURUS HAS SPARKED THE IMAGINATION OF PEOPLE SO MUCH THAT IT WAS
EVEN SUGGESTED THAT IT DID NOT BECOME EXTINCT AND WAS STILL ALIVE
IN PLACES THAT WERE INACCESSIBLE TO HUMANS. AS EVIDENCE OF THIS, A PHOTO
WAS PRODUCED THAT HAD BEEN TAKEN IN 1934 ON THE BANKS OF LOCH NESS IN SCOTLAND,
WHERE A MYSTERIOUS CREATURE SIMILAR TO A PLESIOSAURUS COULD BE SEEN WITH ITS
LONG NECK OUT OF THE WATER AND WHICH LOCALS HAD GIVEN THE NICKNAME NESSIE.
OVER THE YEARS, MANY HAVE TRIED TO FIND THIS ANIMAL BY PROBING THE DEPTHS OF THE LAKE,
BUT OF COURSE, NO ONE HAS EVER FOUND ANY TRACE. THE REASON IS SIMPLE:
PLESIOSAURUS BECAME EXTINCT IN THE LATE CRETACEOUS PERIOD AS THE RESULT
OF THE **CATASTROPHIC IMPACT OF A METEORITE**, THE SAME EVENT
THAT ENDED THE LONG HISTORY OF THE DINOSAURS.

LIOPLEURODON

WHERE IT LIVED:
Europe

WHERE THE MOST IMPORTANT FOSSILS WERE FOUND:
France (Boulogne-sur-Mer and Caen), United Kingdom, Russia

WHEN IT LIVED:
160 to 155 million years ago

SIZE:
from 7 to 10 meters in length

WEIGHT:
between 5 and 15 tons

It was a **VORACIOUS PREDATOR**, one of the most feared among the prehistoric reptiles that inhabited the seas of the planet. Its head measured more than a meter in length and its mouth, **full of sharp protruding teeth**, twice as long as that of a T-Rex, was a terrible deadly weapon. It mainly fed on Ichthyosaurus, Plesiosaurus and large fish which it identified from even tens of kilometers away with its **SENSITIVE NOSE**, capable of analyzing the water in search of the odors of its prey.
It chased them by **swimming quickly thanks to its legs**, which functioned as large oars, and reduced them to pieces with its bite that was powerful enough to kill in seconds.

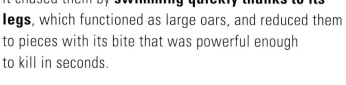

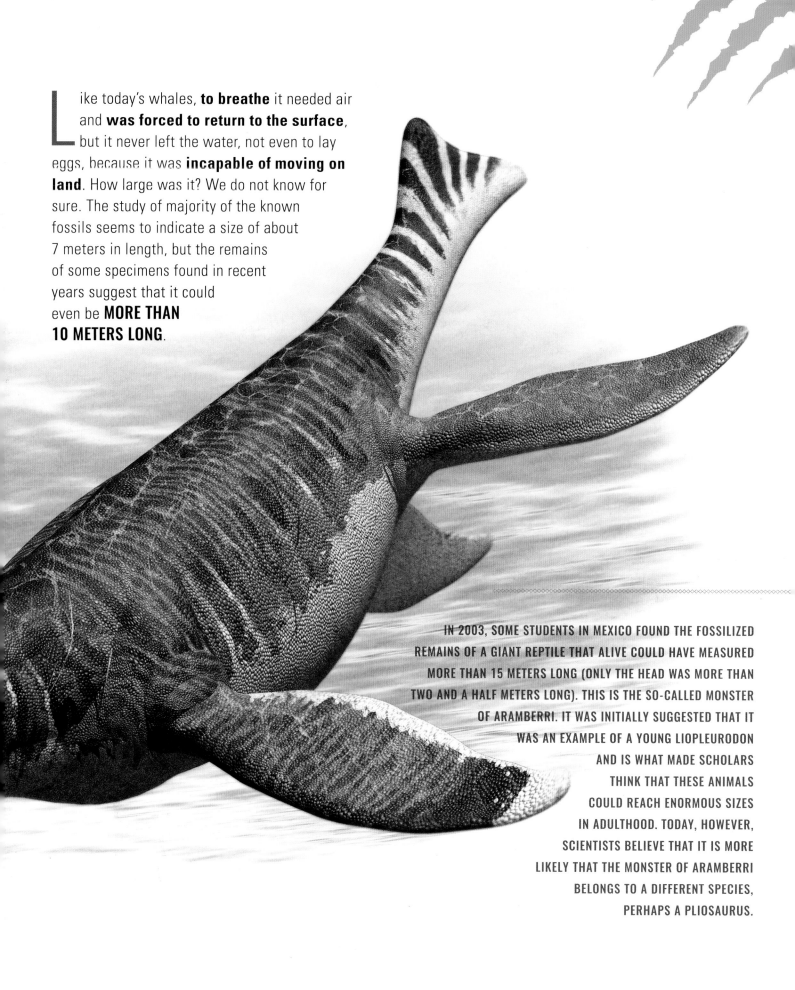

L ike today's whales, **to breathe** it needed air and **was forced to return to the surface**, but it never left the water, not even to lay eggs, because it was **incapable of moving on land**. How large was it? We do not know for sure. The study of majority of the known fossils seems to indicate a size of about 7 meters in length, but the remains of some specimens found in recent years suggest that it could even be **MORE THAN 10 METERS LONG**.

IN 2003, SOME STUDENTS IN MEXICO FOUND THE FOSSILIZED REMAINS OF A GIANT REPTILE THAT ALIVE COULD HAVE MEASURED MORE THAN 15 METERS LONG (ONLY THE HEAD WAS MORE THAN TWO AND A HALF METERS LONG). THIS IS THE SO-CALLED MONSTER OF ARAMBERRI. IT WAS INITIALLY SUGGESTED THAT IT WAS AN EXAMPLE OF A YOUNG LIOPLEURODON AND IS WHAT MADE SCHOLARS THINK THAT THESE ANIMALS COULD REACH ENORMOUS SIZES IN ADULTHOOD. TODAY, HOWEVER, SCIENTISTS BELIEVE THAT IT IS MORE LIKELY THAT THE MONSTER OF ARAMBERRI BELONGS TO A DIFFERENT SPECIES, PERHAPS A PLIOSAURUS.

PLIOSAURUS

WHERE IT LIVED:
In all of the seas on Earth

WHERE THE MOST IMPORTANT FOSSILS WERE FOUND:
Lincolnshire, Oxfordshire (United Kingdom)
and Svalbard (Norway)

WHEN IT LIVED:
160 to 140 million years ago

SIZE:
up to 13 meters in length

WEIGHT:
up to 45 tons

When researchers found the fossilized remains of this dinosaur in the **Arctic archipelago of Svalbard**, they named it **PREDATOR X** (its scientific name is *Pliosaurus funkei*). With a length that would have been around 13 meters, it was **one of the biggest marine reptiles that ever lived**. Its skull, three meters long by itself, contained **a brain that was larger than that of a white shark** in modern times, but the Pliosaurus' aggressiveness was far superior.

iven its size, to not consume too much energy, **it moved slowly**, using only its front fins until it identified its prey. Then, by moving its rear fins, it increased its speed unbelievably until it reached its target. Its **TEETH, MORE THAN 30 CM LONG** and its large jaws gave it a bite that

had **DEVASTATING POWER** (according to scholars, it was four times more powerful than that of a T-Rex). This was how it was able to kill even very large animals without difficulty, animals which it probably **swallowed whole**.

IN 2007, NORWEGIAN PALEONTOLOGISTS HAD ALREADY UNEARTHED A GIGANTIC PLIOSAURUS IN SVALBARD, WHICH THEY HAD CALLED "THE MONSTER." IT DOES NOT TAKE MUCH TO IMAGINE THE REASON FOR THIS NAME. IT WAS 10 TO 12 METERS IN LENGTH AND ITS LEGS, TRANSFORMED INTO FINS, WERE AT LEAST THREE METERS LONG. THIS RECORD WAS THEN SNATCHED AWAY IN 2008 BY THE DISCOVERY OF PREDATOR X. THE BONES OF BOTH SPECIMENS, HOWEVER, DUE TO THE HARSH CLIMATE OF SVALBARD, WERE FRAGMENTED INTO HUNDREDS OF PIECES AND HAS MADE THE JOB OF SCIENTISTS TO REBUILD THEM VERY DIFFICULT, ALMOST AS IF IT WERE A GIANT PUZZLE.